THE
STENCILED
HOUSE

An inspirational and practical guide to transforming your home

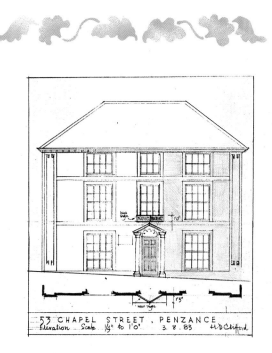

LYN LE GRICE

Photography by
Michael Murray and David Murray

SIMON AND SCHUSTER
New York · London · Toronto · Sydney · Tokyo

For J. and the children

Editorial Amy Carroll

Designed by Bridgewater Design Ltd
Design Peter Bridgewater and Stuart Walden
Line drawings by Rob Shone

Published by Simon and Schuster
A Division of Simon & Schuster Inc.
Simon & Schuster Building
Rockefeller Center
1230 Avenue of the Americas
New York, New York 10020

SIMON AND SCHUSTER and colophon are registered
trademarks of Simon & Schuster Inc.

First published in Great Britain in 1988
by Dorling Kindersley Publishers Limited,
9 Henrietta Street, London WC2E 8PS

Printed and bound in Italy by Mondadori

1   3   5   7   9   10   8   6   4   2

Library of Congress Cataloging in Publication Data

Le Grice, Lyn
    The stenciled house/Lyn Le Grice, photography by Michael Murray
and David Murray.
    p.   cm.
    Includes index.
    ISBN 0-671-66670-3
    1. Stencil work 2. Decoration and ornament 3. Interior
decoration – Amateurs' manuals I. Title.
TT270.L4 1988
745.7'3–dc19

88–15769
CIP

CONTENTS

INTRODUCTION

T HE IMAGERY THAT *surfaces in my stencilwork draws on a store of visual experiences collected throughout my life. Sometimes not fully definable until after the work is complete, it is an almost subconscious process, a flotsam and jetsam of memories selectively recalled and given an airing. An only half-remembered photo of a place in an old color magazine, a mysteriously appealing work of art in a dark corner of a foreign museum, or the quality of the vibrant colors of a piece of old porcelain – all these fleeting visions are dormant, awaiting active recall in all of us.*

THE KITCHEN

Whenever I see a photograph of the interior of Claude Monet's house at Giverny I always admire its style and strong coloring. I think it was my sub conscious memory of the fully-tiled kitchen there that made me first want to attempt the all-over patterned look that I have achieved here in the kitchen in Cornwall. In addition to the more general look of the room, the main thinking behind the design of this room was to draw on its maritime connections. It was, after all, a room in the Old Customs House that served this ancient port of Penzance, and so I have called on nautical paraphernalia to conjure up its stenciled images. The tea clipper comes from the days when Penzance was a starting-off point for those amazingly fast voyages carried out by exceptionally graceful vessels on their journeys to and from the Indies. The anchor speaks for itself as an all-time symbol for activities at sea, and I worked from an ancient map for the design of the compass. The ship's bell over the small door sports a suitably convoluted nautical knot and the huge rope derives from the great coils of rope that litter the quays of the harbors throughout the world.

THE HALL

The imagery in the hall is drawn from rare handpainted wallpaper, occasionally found lining the boudoirs of grand houses of the eighteenth century. There is a lovely room in Chatsworth embellished in this manner where the Chinese shrubs and foliage seem to actually grow up the walls. I looked at such interiors closely before working on the stencils for this hall area. The drawings of the shrubs have benefitted from my firsthand experience and love of Cornish gardens.

The birds are also taken from old imported Chinese wallpapers. Yellow was an appropriate color for these birds, and worked in great harmony with the delicate blue coloring of the walls and the stronger, exotic coloring of the shrubs. The languid bases to these trees, however, are influenced by the more naive early American renditions of plainer trees. The slightly overscaled butterflies in the hall derive from early botanical prints and have little in common with butterflies as we know them on our shores today; they are more like the exotic species from South America.

The stenciling of the little hall just outside the bedrooms is of simple little leaves sprigged across the walls with a single leaf on each of the upper panels of the three small doors. I feel it to be something of a tribute to the Brontës whose mother was born in a fine little square brick house close by – a few houses on down in the same road, towards the sea.

THE PARLOR

The illusion of a much grander hall paved with great stone slabs set with slate, has been captured in humble paintwork here. A chintz border runs around the outside of this slabbed area. In fact, while not entirely appropriate, perhaps a slightly punchier design might have been more apt, particularly in a larger room. However, in a small room, I think one gets away with the delicacy of this design. It is taken from the same source as the imagery behind the rest of the room, which is that of those toile de vie prints produced in the taste of Marie Antoinette. They are usually little vignettes of rural scenes and are interspersed across the surface of chintz and wallpaper in monochrome. The cloth has been treated entirely in that way, although more airily spaced than the original to give it a more naive feel. The cameos of the various small animals that are stenciled into the centers of the panels of the room repeat this same feeling although they also borrow something from woodcuts done by Berwick.

THE DINING ROOM

The design of the dining room relies on the ancient and venerable device, the vine. This has been repeatedly used throughout the ages, employed to decorate all manner of surfaces and artifacts. The curving shape of the ceiling conjured up for me the image of an old vine-clad arbor, the kind one would stroll under for shade in the gardens of some French chateau, and this suggested, too, the hooping across the barrel of the ceiling. A recent early viewing of some newly uncovered stenciling at Pentyre was also inspirational. Here, one of the upper rooms of an ancient manor house, had sections revealed to expose bold and beautiful stencilwork, and the sight of this work, meticulously uncovered by its present owner, led me to the conclusion that the dining room of the house would be most suitable to be adorned with a vine.

THE SITTING ROOM

The stenciling here is derived at first sight from the same source as the hall – the tree sprouting from the tufted earth. But in the sitting room, my direct inspiration was that of Jacobean crewelwork and its magnificent flowering tree of life. The most exuberant needlework, usually taking the form of bed or chair coverings, was created in this period. I have greatly relished studying such work, in varying conditions of decay, for quite often these tapestries are the subject of restoration by the various schools of needlework and specialist restoration departments. These luxuriant growths support all manner of fruit, flower and foliage and when looking at the various kinds, the character of the executor comes through loud and clear. A form of needlework that predates crewelwork is that of stumpwork. It is the most beautiful kind of needlework with its raised and padded shapes embellished with metal thread and sequins and very frequently repeated. Unfortunately few examples remain, but some very special designs survive in Trerice, a National Trust house in Cornwall. There you can quite often see small designs repeated but in different positions on the work as a whole. There is also some very beautiful stumpwork at the Dorset Country Museum, at Dorchester. This is where I first saw it, and got intrigued by it. Depicted in this manner are goddesses of the harvest, deer, monkeys and tigers, and at the same size, greatly enlarged, insects and butterflies.

THE PAISLEY BEDROOM

I have looked at books on the Kashmir shawl and compiled a lot of patterns for this room. There are many different forms within such imagery and the main excitement is in building up the borders, one upon another, to eventually end up with a powerfully serpentining main theme, a typical paisley form interspersed with smaller leaves. Gothic architecture was another influence on this room; the curved dagging of the cornices echo a typical gothic arch. I used these arches to impose a stronger style on the windows than that of their plain straightforward Georgian construction. Another stylistic feature imposed on this room is the marquetry look of the floor. It resembles the beautifully blocked floors of far grander buildings, such as European palaces.

THE BATHROOM

Here, I have been influenced by yet another period of style – the twenties/ thirties, and I think that the striped bunting that rings the tops of the walls in this room recalls designers, such as Oliver Messel, who were working in the 1930's. The whole room has somehow slipped into this period. Paisley is also strongly present here with its beguiling Indian design borrowed so freely by the Europeans.

The coloring of this room is Caribbean, and it records a visit to my brother's house which was on one of those bright islands; a momento of the most incredible color of the sea there. There is more formal decoration on the cupboard which is painted to simulate marble with straight trees infilling the panels. The influence here came from an Indian cupboard that I saw in Country Life magazine many years ago. It was elaborately inlaid with ivory palm trees and stayed in my mind. The stenciling of the baskets on top of the cupboard has more to do with a modern-day influence – products from Hong Kong or the Philippines – effective souvenirs for the tourists. The demure sprigged muslin used on the screens probably is more reminiscent of Jane Austen than the Roaring Twenties.

THE SAMPLER BEDROOM

The sampler bedroom, as with the sitting room, draws strongly on a particular form of needlework that was displayed on the intriguingly varied samplers worked in the nineteenth century and earlier. Love of a particular sampler that belonged to my Grandmother and now, most fortunately, belongs to me, is basically behind the main border design. I later tell of the origin of the amusing panels of each month worked in cross stitch by the Queen of Denmark. They tell the story of a couple meeting throughout the year and take the form of a calendar book. The many other motifs on the bed and canopy curtains come from samplers of many decades, one in particular that was appropriate to this area – the lobster on the bedcover. The yellow chest in the same room has a less robust edition of crewelwork stenciled all over its curving top and sides while the Adam and Eve on the front are derived from one of the most classical of images.

THE DAY NURSERY

For this play room I have drawn strongly on my own memories of illustrations in nursery rhyme books, pored over and familiar to my childhood. I remember being particularly involved with the beautiful little tree with its silver nutmeg and golden pear. This was endorsed at a later stage when reading to my children about a princess who was greatly intrigued by a similar little tree that was the sole possession of a humble gardener's boy. She desired this tree above all else, and in the end, after much turmoil, a great friendship was forged, based on the mutual love and care of this tree. The little tools crossed on the doors of the cupboard come also from the memory of the miniature tools that the princess and the gardener's boy used and fought over when they tended the tree in the palace garden.

The shells placed around the baseboards of the room give the room the feeling of a garden, and I remember thinking what a very attractive idea it was to have shells edging your flower beds; however ideas and influences evolve and, luckily, mature. For example, the prettiness of the rings of roses and the bows on the bells come from an early unashamed desire for prettiness before one learned to be more wary. The richness of the coloring of the sky and stars on the ceiling derive from the many interpretations of the night of the Nativity (strangely intermixed with the "Man in the Moon" I think from an old Ovaltine advertisement).

THE NIGHT NURSERY

The influence for the night nursery comes from those little unpretentious upper rooms in Swedish houses. The painted gray floor, and the cool calm imagery of the leaves and ribbons in this room, in my mind, come directly from the whole feeling one has from Swedish interiors, and it was my aim to create such a setting of calm clarity. Furniture was kept simple and to a minimum. The use of canvas floor coverings was once very popular in England, too. Sadly, this charming concept is hardly seen these days.

THE
FURNITURE

There is something very memorable about a piece of furniture that is decorated with paintwork images; it attracts our attention and its pictures appeal to the child in us. There are few rooms that are not enlivened by the addition of some such piece, however elaborately decorated. It is in spartan surroundings, however, that this furniture finds the very best foil. In such places, a highly decorated armoire, for instance, would look splendid giving a room a focus and a heart.

It is not difficult with the aid of stencils to create highly satisfying effects on furniture that, before its transformation, appeared mundane. Most of the pieces illustrated on the proceeding pages were plain to the point of boredom, and certainly would have turned no attentive heads.

It is not always necessary to paint the surface of furniture to be stenciled – sometimes the color of the wood is lovely and its markings too fine to cover. It could also be that your subject is painted in a good color already; don't be put off by the odd sign of wear, this should be welcomed and left as it is. It is extremely difficult to create such a patina with new paint, and it always makes a more sensitive surface to stencil on.

When working out the look you wish to create with your stencils do bear in mind that the main appeal of the old painted furniture lay mainly, not with its subject matter, nor with the degree of its design complexity, but with its engaging fusing of colors. It has to be said, however, that it is with the subject matter that the more overt appeal lies. But be wary; no matter how strong this attraction, it can be killed stone dead by an interpretation carried out in raucous colors applied over harshly printed surfaces.

On the following pages I've shown how to stencil a selection of furniture. Kitchen chairs make a fine subject for a first stencil project. Traditionally, the areas to decorate are the backs and seats. Tabletops of almost any size can be used like horizontal panels on which one can either decorate with restraint or indulge in something more full blown. A blanket chest presents a good broad canvas for decoration, enough to tell a whole story, and a chest of drawers enables one to distribute a pattern over a large, often broken surface, to good effect.

The undistinguished plainly painted chest of drawers that once filled the alcove of the old fireplace has been transformed into a highly decorative piece. On the mantlepiece above is the traditional ornate bread made for the harvest festival, depicting the five loaves and two fishes of the parable.

THE CHAIR

Chairs are seldom accorded the respect due to their finely balanced constructions that are built to withstand the wear and tear of daily life. However, treated to a little stencilwork, they will repay the attention handsomely.

For this slat-backed kitchen chair I designed a sheaf of barley to lie across the top of its curved back and another – larger and crescent-shaped – to follow the subtle indentation on its seat.

I chose the less than natural coloring of the blues purely because they heightened the rich background of wood. After it was painted, I burnished up the surface with a good wax polish and the design instantly seemed more at home.

1 The first step in stenciling is planning out your design on paper. Here are my sketches for the seat and back bar of the kitchen chair.

2 Using pencil, I then transferred the designs to be appropriately-cut pieces of stencil card.

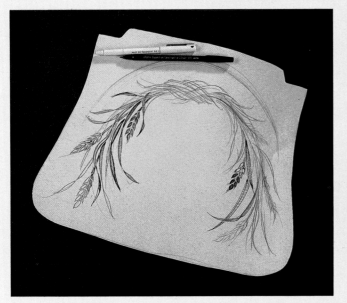

3 Having changed to a felt-tip pen, I began working out the design in more detail, specifically separating out the different shapes.

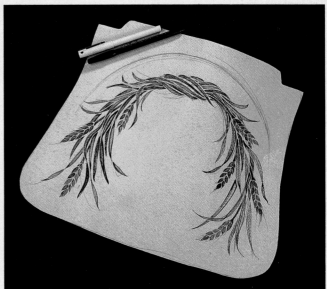

4 Once the outline of the designs were defined, I blocked them in with cross-hatching for further clarity.

5 I began to cut away the blocked-in areas leaving sufficient width between each cut shape. These widths, known as bridges, also form part of the design.

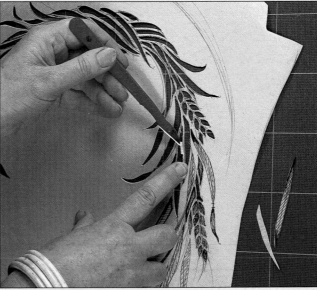

6 When a knife mistakenly cuts through one of the bridges between two cut-away shapes, mend it on both sides with a narrow strip of masking tape.

7 I slashed the top of the stencil to accommodate the curve of the chair back. It was fixed with spray adhesive and held with masking tape.

8 I attached the seat stencil and masked off the areas surrounding the stencils that might catch some spray with two pieces of card.

9 I sprayed the leaf color and used a curved guard, held over the heads of the grain, to prevent that color from spreading onto them.

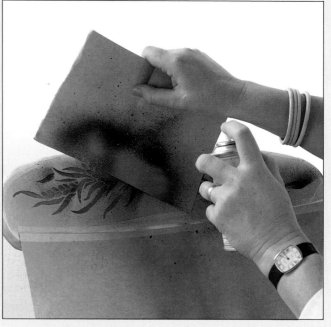

10 Then I sprayed the gold color for the grain and used a guard to protect the leaves from the gold.

TOP On the finished chair, the colors blend well with the rich background of the wood grain.

RIGHT The detail of the chair back shows the darker colors covering the paler first coat.

THE TABLE

Borders always look stylish on table tops giving extra emphasis to basic shapes, so one should be utilized, even if it is just a broken line.

This little nondescript table, coated as it was in a brown gravy-colored varnish, presented a disguised but promising face. Its plain straight legs could also use some attention. A covering of my favorite soft gray paint was smudged across its surface, not entirely obliterating the darker tones underneath.

The small, unadorned side table is very uninteresting but should be much improved by the addition of some stenciling.

I envisaged a ribbony posy design and drew it with its border skirting the outer edge of the table top by approximately one inch.

A long strip of the unfolding ribbon border was also used to stencil the legs and cross struts. I used a good bright blue color for the ribbon that, coupled with the pink flowers of the posy, produced an overtly pretty impression.

1 Next to my original sketch is the cut-out stencil for the table top. The border stencil that will be applied to the legs and edges is drawn, ready for cutting.

2 The bottom corner had to be reattached to the main stencil. It was cut away in order to spray it through onto the other 3 corners for identical cutting.

3 The drawn-in border designs flow into one another at the corners. The bridges, of equal size, are placed at regular intervals to contribute to the tempo.

4 I added depth to the design by spraying a darker color onto the underlapping sections of the ribbon. A guard protects the paler top portions.

5 The border stencil is fixed in position on the side edge of the table and demonstrates the linking with the stenciling going down the leg.

6 The effectiveness of deeply shading the ribbon folds is clearly seen on the completed tabletop design.

THE BLANKET CHEST

If a table presents a good broad canvas for decoration, a solid rectangular blanket chest presents many more – enough to tell a whole story.

This repetition of images is, of course, what one is always looking for when designing for this craft, and here I was able to repeat not only the camels, but also the palms and the distant simplified pyramids.

2 The stencils for the front and sides are partially cut out. The area between the two trees on the smaller stencil allows for the protruding handle.

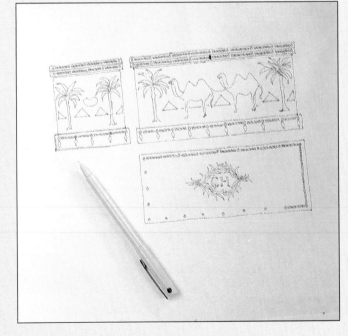

1 My sketch for the blanket chest had the design distributed over its front, top and sides.

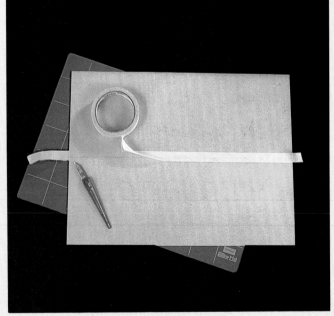

3 My design for the top was of such a scale that it was necessary to join two pieces of card. I butted them up together and taped across.

4 *Into the center of the wreath, I placed the initials of the Customs House. The thin layer of masking tape was cut through as I removed the leaves.*

5 *The separate border stencil was used on the first half of the top and then reversed and fixed into position to complete its rectangle on the lid.*

THE CHEST OF DRAWERS

The only interesting thing about this unadorned chest of drawers was its drawer formation – a little central drawer at the top flanked by two smaller drawers with two long shallow drawers at the base. I began by covering the plain white paint with a coat of Indian red enamel and then covered this with a coat of glossy black.

2 A set of the stencils sketched out and subsequently cut for the top, bottom drawer and framing at each side of the chest of drawers.

1 My original sketch shows stenciling on the drawer fronts only. I later added stenciling to the side borders. The drawing at the bottom is for the top.

3 The stencils are now complete, the border edging is there, and cut out. Notice how I had to cut one of the stencils to fit around the knobs.

4 The most attractive stencilwork integrates well with structural features. Notice how the design curves naturally around the knobs and corners.

5 A repeat of the simpler sheaf of wheat used on the second drawer works well on the glowing black enamel surface of the top of the chest.

6 The basket of eggs is placed securely at the base of the bottom drawer, while the second drawer displays a complementary but simpler motif.

7 The finished chest of drawers shows the balance that is necessary to achieve the distribution of pattern over the different surfaces of furniture.

THE
KITCHEN

T HIS LOFTY OLD *kitchen is located at the back of the house and has that sort of spaciousness that reminds one that it was the workplace for several people – a cook and various helpers. Here, they performed such tasks as sorting groceries, preparing the food, general cleaning, and washing up. From here, too, they would have overseen the overall running of the house and used this room as the starting point for the running up and down of stairs to attend to the numerous rooms.*

THE ROOM'S PHYSICAL
FEATURES

The kitchen does, in fact, provide the sort of area in which quite a number of people can work in harmony together. For instance, it easily accommodates the enormous old kitchen table that is of a scale that would be very difficult to fit into any of the larger rooms of the average home. However, the most stunning feature of this room is the ancient window that is of such an age that one questions not just the year but the century of its origin.

To one side, in the form of a support, is a great tree trunk which, in a windswept penninsula like this, most probably originated as the mast of a ship. There are very few trees from this part of the world that have trunks of that size.

To the left of the opposite window there was a very narrow alcove set into the wall – the sort of space to house a 1930's gas stove. When we excavated this area a very friendly old brick fire-

place emerged, exactly what one hopes to discover in old houses like this. Brick fireplaces are quite unusual for Cornwall; mostly, down here, they are constructed of granite. This one is all mellow brick with that lovely patch-work of different tones, some with cream, some the usual soft red, dark and blackened. A giant mantlepiece was contrived to be of a scale to do justice to an opening of this size, and so a thick plank was found and hauled up into place, supported by some very solid mantles of wood which my younger son carved, with a suitably rough Cornish shield to which he added a rugged scroll at the base of each angle.

A chest of drawers stands in the fireplace alcove at present. This is painted a shiny black and has a very pretty drawer formation; a little central drawer at the top flanked by two smaller drawers with two long shallow drawers at the base. On these I have stenciled in rich warm colors. On the lowest drawer sits a basket of eggs in a bed of bracken and grasses. I have put

Lunchtime in the kitchen with a tureen of turnip soup on the table which is set next to the window seat. Early Cornish daffodils and anemones brighten this spring table and look well with the blue of the stenciled walls.

a little frieze of interwoven grasses flanking each side while sheaves of grasses decorate other drawers and the top. It has the look of a lacquered tea cannister and shows up the effectiveness of stenciling on a darker color. In order to get the colors to glow as they have, when I placed the stencil on the chest, first I sprayed the whole of the exposed area with a film of white paint, so that the other paints that I applied then sat on this white paint and I could make it deeper and lighter. This meant that I wasn't working on the dense black of the chest

when applying the other lighter colors. This is something to remember when stenciling on darker tones.

Another intriguing feature of this room is a remnant of one of the seemingly numerous old staircases of the house. (This time it meets at the base of a cemented-up wall, where it once would have led into a neighboring building); yet another of these escape routes built into this historic old house. I wonder quite what did go on here because of the number of staircases that we have found. This staircase opens into the room above through a trap door, and so leads to nowhere. It does, however, form the

most decorative angle to the corner of the room flanking the fireplace.

The floor of this room was probably only earth before it had concrete poured over it. It is now cracked and uneven but very friendly, and so we checkered it up into big flagstones of terracotta and a deep, dark slatey blue. Surrounding this boldly is an enormous indigo blue rope border. We waxed it until we got the patina that we wished. It now seems strong and clear, a spacious expanse, complementing the complexity of the room as a whole. Its square formality brings a little order to the room which is basically made up of a podge hodge of the building carried out through the various centuries of its existence.

The ceiling is divided by a large beam, the base of which just appears through the old plaster ceiling. This is very useful for hanging and fixing various things such as lanterns, clothes and herbs to dry and probably, in its time, had the odd ham hanging from one of its hooks.

There is a piece of my early stenciling in this room. It is the chair with the life-like fox slinking across the top slat of its back.

The chairs around the table have got clasps of corn on their curved backs. I have used mostly blue, not the expected gold, for these motifs because blue looks so well against the tanned color of the chairs, although this is highlighted by a very pale gold on the heads of barley. The seats also have a clasp of corn curving into their cutaway concave shape.

The stencilwork on both the chairs and the fireplace chest of drawers was described in detail in the previous chapter.

OPPOSITE The kitchen stencils with the blue spray paint across them, their work complete.

LEFT An old stairway slices through the corner of this wall interrupting its wall decoration. The floor with illusionary tiles and stenciled with a bold rope border in deepest navy.

As one goes further on around the room, there is a very delightful little Victorian door that leads through into the hall, and next to this there is an area showing traces of an opening for another fire. It has long ago been blocked up and as we have already found an enormous fireplace in this room, we felt that was enough, and we left the wall intact, resisting the urge to excavate.

Deeply recessed, next to the old window (and shown overleaf) is a quite beautiful door, the period of which is difficult to judge, but it is one of the loveliest doors of the house and hangs from the most substantial pair of hinges. A lot of its appeal is that it is so deeply set into this very thick wall.

Near to the door is the first chest that I ever stenciled – my husband's old tool chest. Its original deep battle-ship gray paint, still adhering to parts of it, appealed to me. Years ago I stenciled this surface with some tur-quoise blue rings of leaves and some plain round oranges and blossoms. The crudeness with which I tackled this piece is something that at times I wish I hadn't lost and could retrieve. With time one gets a little too able with a craft, and you don't achieve the bold clarity with which the first naive jobs were approached. However there are other times when I look at this and think how incredibly crude and ugly it is, so I suppose it is just a question of deciding where one stands and in the end being prepared to encompass the lot, or questions get too complicated.

OPPOSITE *The rough texture of the original paintwork of this chest can be seen behind the stenciled garland.*

LEFT *The stenciling on this chest was my very first attempt at this ancient craft. From this point I became enslaved. (It has a lot to answer for.) It is surprising how amiably it merges with the diagonally patterned stenciling behind it, and it sits most comfortably on the blandly stenciled floor. The floor has similarities with the one in the picture above the chest, of an early American interior.*

THE STENCIL SCHEME

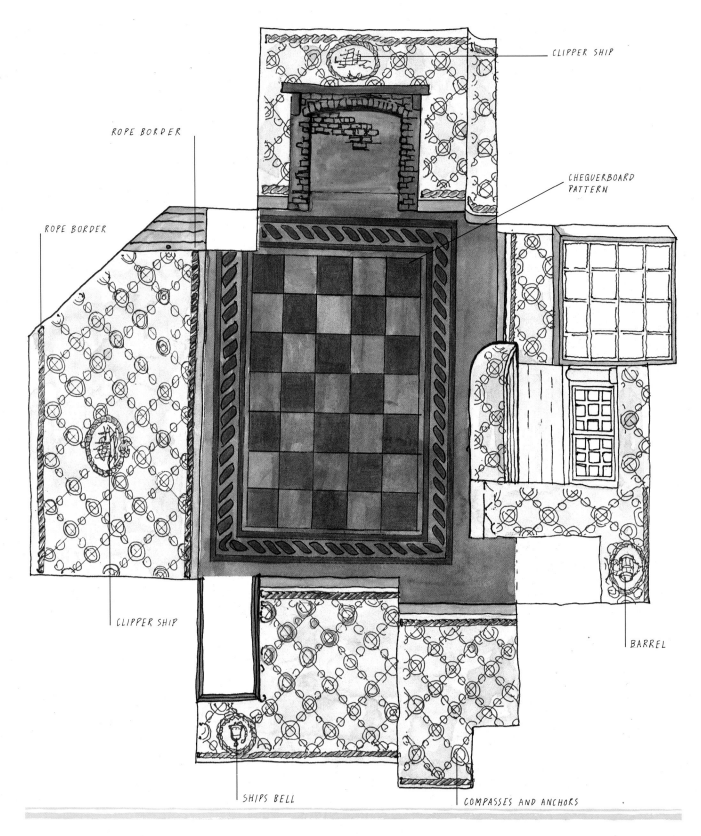

ROPE BORDER

CLIPPER SHIP

ROPE BORDER

CHEQUERBOARD PATTERN

CLIPPER SHIP

BARREL

SHIPS BELL

COMPASSES AND ANCHORS

THE DESIGN SCHEME

Because this was the Old Customs House serving the harbor of Penzance, it seemed that somewhere one should select this aspect of its former existence in its decoration, and so the theme for the kitchen is specifically maritime. It also gave me the excuse to use the traditional fresh coloring of the sea, blue and white. The whole surface of the main wall has been stenciled with rope rings encircling anchors, compasses, less generally a tea clipper, a ship's bell and a barrel on its hauling tackle. These last items have been strategically placed in particular areas of the room. For instance, above the entrance to the room is a large oval of rope in which is suspended, perhaps rather mena-cingly, the barrel with its chain, looking as if it has just been hoisted off a ship. Maybe it is a barrel of brandy. The ship's bell is placed above the little Victorian door in a circle of rope, while the *pièce de résistance* is centrally placed over the mantlepiece – a full rigged tea clipper under sail. This is repeated in a central position on the main wall. The blue that I have chosen is not the sort of strong butcher blue that one would expect but verging on indigo, gently suggesting a link with the sea. I have squared up the walls diagonally in order to make the anchors interspersed with the compass, which are the main repeating motifs, spread right across the whole of these walls to form a large-scale lattice work. These give the look of a totally tiled room.

TOP The barrel on its hoisting chain hangs slightly ominously over the deeply set kitchen door. It has the same oval rope frame as the tea clipper.

RIGHT The speeding tea clipper is placed in the middle of the main kitchen wall surrounded by numerous anchors and compasses. It also takes the central position above the fireplace.

THE WINDOWS

The most interesting window has a complex construction that includes many panes of glass which are variously engraved. One of the panes is scratched with the name Ben – undated so unfortunately we don't know at what period he sat in this window making his mark. There is also, hatched onto one of these panes, the profile of a face. There are some other much more recent markings: The name of F.B. Edmonds is executed with a great flourish of copper-plate lettering. Was this inscribed with a diamond? Other panes are of Victorian glass that are situated unevenly across its different levels and have been frosted with a lace-like pattern.

The window has a very deep window ledge and its two different sides – which must have, at one time, slid over each other to open – are now quite statically embedded into the complex casing of each window. The whole structure bows out noticeably in the middle.

An appealing window seat stretches below this window with a backing of old planks which join up to the uneven sill. This varies in depth from about 4″ at one end to 2″ at the other, and, as if this isn't enough, it is on two levels. The complete lack of any particularly formal squaring up of the house in general is epitomized here with this window, and its surrounding architecture. This window is not large but it is very dominant in the room.

TOP There is a marked contrast in scale and style between the two kitchen windows. The great charm of this ancient window lies in its totally informal make-up; propped, as it is one end, on a great mast of a tree trunk, it is neither straight nor level.

LEFT The big window in the kitchen reaches up to the ceiling and lets in the morning sunlight. Its three tiers of checkered curtains break up its height to a more domestic scale and lend warmth on grayer days.

THE
PARLOR

J UST OFF *the entrance corridor on the ground floor is a pretty, cozy little room that serves as a parlor. This room may possibly have been the office when the building was the Customs House. Several details I've uncovered, see below, lead me to that opinion. I decided in this room, that there was little more one could add to it in terms of the sheer appeal of the panels, so I decided to concentrate on the decoration of the floor.*

THE DESIGN CONCEPT

A painted and stenciled floor for such a room seemed entirely appropriate, and has indeed turned out to be so. It gives what, in fact, is quite a small room of very average dimensions, an extra spaciousness which is achieved by the spacing out of these checkered markings across the floor, so that at whatever part you are standing in the room you see this vista of squares stretching ahead of you.

I planned to enclose these squared, paved-off parts with a blown-up edition of the border which we could also use in the room on textiles. It was important for me to scale up the design to make it work for the floor. When you decorate floors, because of their size, you must think in a different scale. If you try to work with a border as intimate as if you were decorating a piece of furniture, you would end up with something much too intricate and very bitty. You have to think in a broader and bolder way, and then you have to apply the whole design with a much more definite hand.

The walls and fabrics of the room were to be stenciled with a theme of English field animals. In the finished room, you can see the chosen images. There is a fairly large stencil of a fox, padding rather purposefully, through slightly marshy ground and under a rather wizened oak tree, to look for goodness knows what – one of the little field mice probably. On the door of the old staircase in the top panel we do have a field mouse crouching under some barley and amongst some pebbles. On the bottom panel there is a hedgehog nosing his way through some more stony ground. There is a weasel up and alert and listening amongst some more grassy patches and another bit of oak tree; and a very contented squirrel up in a swinging branch of another oak. Finally an otter appears, sneaking along the banks of some shallow water. Again there is the repeated motif of the oak tree and its leaves filling out the shape to make a fuller design for the panel. I have also used tufts of grass on some of these panels where I felt it was justified to create a nicer shape.

A corner of the parlor which shows the way part of the border design is left out in order to accommodate the hearthstone.

THE ROOM'S PHYSICAL FEATURES

The parlor walls are simply paneled in wood above an imposing dado rail. Deep baseboards surround the planked floor. There is a pretty plaster cornice around the ceiling, and the whole of the room has enormous charm, both because of its paneling and its shape, and there is just a very good feeling in it. The fireplace is particularly elegant – another of our crooked fireplaces which I have become so fond of here – but the structure of it is extremely refined for such a humble little room.

The fireplace itself is Victorian, but it has gracious broad sweeps and rather fine detailing, with a lovely criss-cross design outside, all of cast iron.

The window is in a deep recess, and has paneling all around it as well as paneled shutters. There is a strange change of scale at the window level where the window goes up a little higher than the actual ceiling of the room. This is because of the Georgian facade added more recently to the front of the house. It also means that when you look out of this window which directly gives out on to the street, you are actually looking at a street level higher than the levels of the floor of the room. All these strange levels seem to fit in and add to the great charm of the room.

So in addition to the totally paneled room, we have a very charmingly paneled alcove for the window and an elegant little fireplace on one side. More interestingly, there is a strange little door, which now fronts a cupboard, but which used to provide access to the old staircase of the house. When you open the door, you can still see the first three steps of that old staircase sitting in the bottom of the cupboard. It is a much earlier staircase than the grander staircase that was put in later, and it always gives me a special thrill to see it and imagine the uses it

Otter

Badger

Fox

Squirrel

Hedgehog

Weasel

Mouse

Border

38

had. Maybe it was a secondary staircase, used at the time when it was the Customs House.

Set into the wall next to the door there is a large cupboard which has four elegant panels to its top part. Inside, when you open the door, you can see little cubic spaces. Although I can't work it out, I believe they have something to do with the work of the old customs men. They are almost like letter racks, but not quite long enough. Perhaps they held different flags or certificates – I don't know, but I can imagine many things from such details. It's a very interesting old cupboard, disguised below the dado rail as wall, and next to it is a very pretty little glass windowed door.

Finally, there is a long stretch of wall with four elegant panels. This to me, really is the essence of the room's elegance.

Deceptively large in the photographs, the Parlor measures a mere 10 feet by 13 feet 9 inches. The ceiling height is 7 feet 6 inches. The stenciled decoration is quite restrained on the walls; it is the painted floor that is the room's chief glory.

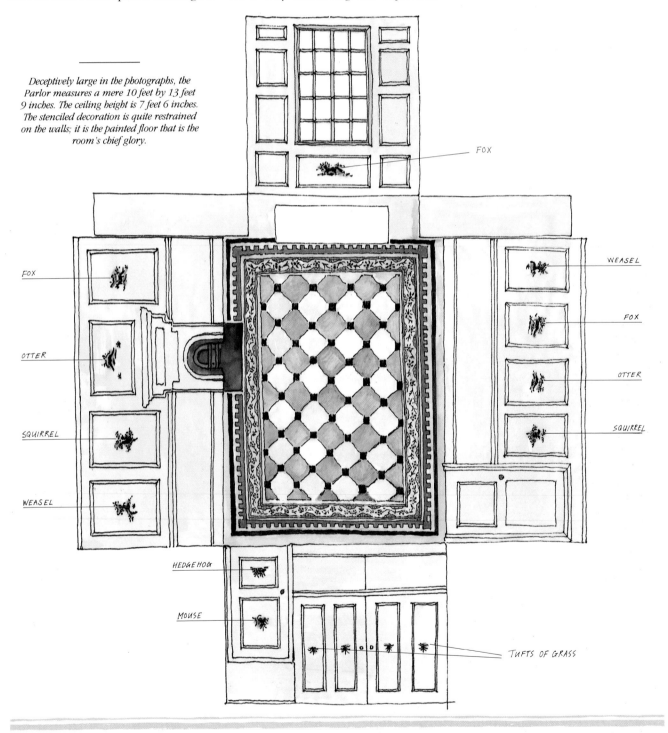

FOX

FOX

OTTER

SQUIRREL

WEASEL

WEASEL

FOX

OTTER

SQUIRREL

HEDGEHOG

MOUSE

TUFTS OF GRASS

THE DECORATIVE
TREATMENT

We wanted to control the coloring, so we used the same color for the floor as for the walls, in order to add to the whole spacious feeling. If you break up a color between one plane and another, you are actually enclosing it more, and by just letting the whole color wash across both the walls and floor of this room (the ceiling itself is just traditional white, which I must say I find hard to beat), you actually do achieve an extra feeling of space. I wanted to use very warm terracotta colors against the quite strict black and gray of the rest of the floor coloring. I've used just terracotta for the painted stenciled panels. We used an old traditional sailcloth canvas from the local sailmakers loft to cover a chaise longue. This we have stenciled very sparingly just around the skirt of

its cover. The rest of the cover just has some terracotta piping.

Scattered across this chaise longue, which is set into the window recess, we have made a number of cushions of different shapes, but all with imagery that has been used in the room. Each cushion contains a separate animal: sometimes he is just sitting there alone in the middle of a panel; sometimes he has the calico border around him. There is an infinite variety of ways that you can use these patterns to create a cushion effect and these are just four of them. The cushions have introduced another color, a rather extravagant emerald green, which just gives a freshness to that particular vignette of the chaise longue in the alcove.

The window cloth looks like an old French Toile de Jouy design. The glazed calico is bordered down each of the edges with a more delicate version of the pattern used so boldly around the

ABOVE The otter lurks at the water's edge in the panel above the fireplace.

RIGHT The elaborately stenciled floor contrasts with the more controlled treatment of the wall panels which display a single animal stenciled in one coloring.

floor. Crowded between these patterned borders are the images of all the different animals. They are all painted in one color – terracotta – on to the natural color of the glazed chintz. Grasses are interspersed between the animals to add a rhythm.

In the corner of the room there is a round table covered with a stenciled tablecloth. The cloth has the same animals strewn across it, and because of the rounded edge, I cut the border into a slight curve so that we were able to go all around the edge and gradually make that curve work. In such a clear, plain room as this, with its beautiful paneling, you are able to slightly emphasize the imagery that you do put in, and use it in more ways than if you had other patterns existing in the room. So it is the plainness of the room that allows you to use the same pattern, although it is in a different scale, several times over, without the room feeling over-decorated.

The wooden furniture in the room is rather yellowy in tone, and is complicated by the coloring of the log basket. Some basketwork boxes sit on the table, which have this lovely terracotta color mingled with the plain basketwork color. Also about the room are old books, a clock and lamps. Some elegant figurines of two gardeners stand on the mantlepiece each side of a little pastille burner. On the table is a rather extraordinary dish on a stand. The little desk has a lamp, a marquetry box made to look like books, some chessmen and a pewter inkstand.

ABOVE A small mouse sits in a bright frame of green tenting canvas.

LEFT When standing in this humble but elegant room, there is a very real feeling of spaciousness.

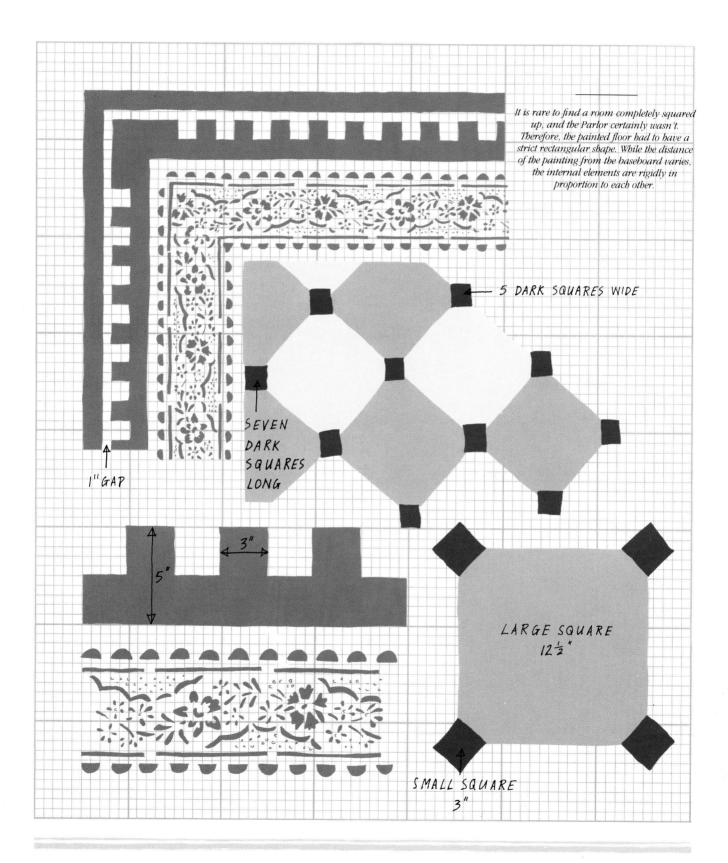

It is rare to find a room completely squared up, and the Parlor certainly wasn't. Therefore, the painted floor had to have a strict rectangular shape. While the distance of the painting from the baseboard varies, the internal elements are rigidly in proportion to each other.

5 DARK SQUARES WIDE

SEVEN DARK SQUARES LONG

1" GAP

3"

5"

LARGE SQUARE 12½"

SMALL SQUARE 3"

STENCILING THE FLOOR

I made sure I always had a minimum distance of 6″ from the baseboard, but the maximum was variable. The border width, some 18″ was marked out from the outer edge of this rectangle, leaving a smaller inner rectangle.

Working out from the center point the floor, with its angular tile effect, was marked out using masking tape.

The small intermediate "tiles" were sprayed first and then the larger gray ones. The main border was applied in three different stages. First, a plain black line 1½″ thick was sprayed between two parallel strips of masking tape. Second, the castellated border was applied 1″ width away from the plain black line. Third, an enlarged version of the Calico border was laid 1″ distant from the castellated border. This also was colored Indian red, and highlighted with a rich yellow ocher. This border fell 1″ short of meeting the inner rectangle of "tiles" already in place. The whole surface was then given a complete coat of protective polyurethane varnish to ensure a hard-wearing surface.

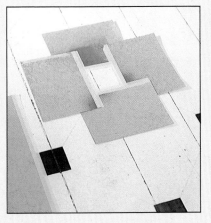

1 Once the whole floor was painted, I masked off the squares for the small intermediate tiles, using pieces of card. These were then densely sprayed black.

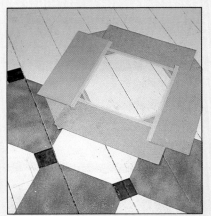

2 I then masked off the shapes for the larger tiles (having first protected the small black ones). These were given a more mottled texture by using two different shades of gray.

3 The border pattern consisted of 2 separate stencils. I began by putting down the castellated border. This was painted Indian red.

4 Here I show how the castellated border pieces are aligned using tape. When this border was all sprayed, I followed with the calico border.

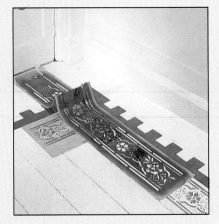

5 To make the design flow as it reached the corner and turned to meet another length of border, I sprayed from each direction onto a clean strip of stencil card.

6 I left the actual corner bare of design so I could draw new shapes fusing the common elements to complete the design.

7 The new shapes had to be cut away and sprayed onto the corner of the floor. Then the straight borders were sprayed up to meet them before applying the varnish.

THE
HALL AND STAIRWAY

ONE ENTERS *the Customs House through the Regency porch surrounding the front door with its supporting pillars on each side, then on into a little low passageway. At the end of the passage with a couple of doors leading off it, you suddenly walk into the hall and stairwell, the area from which one can look up and see right at the top of the house between its three floors. The intimate narrowness of the passage makes this all the more startling, and people seldom fail to gasp as they walk in and suddenly see the real scale of the house, not detectable from its facade. The compact squareness that one sees from the street leads back into a rambling old house with seventeen rooms.*

When you come to the end of the passage you have only reached the middle of the house. The staircase forms a central core through the house with doors leading off it on every floor.

I find the staircase something of a parody in the way it reflects so closely the complex nature of the whole building. It is indeed a very convoluted structure, encompassing a variety of styles. It has grown organically with the house.

At the head of the stairs on the top floor, outside the children's nursery rooms, the staircase is a very sturdy, possibly Jacobean structure, that is very formal and squared, and at this stage it is quite narrow. But if one proceeds down the stairs onto a curving sort of structure that feels a bit like a captain's bridge, one is suspended in the very center of the stairwell. The railings and the handrail suddenly become something far more Victorian, very fluid and very simple. At this stage, the stairs widen out quite con-

siderably and the solid central structure that is the earlier part ends on the first floor.

The staircase then hugs the wall as it curves around graciously outside the main sitting room and the dining room doors, and then leads along a galleried walk to reach the wall on the far side. It again is wide and comes down in a more formal squared-off way, hugging the edge of the main stairwell. The structure of the ballustrading here is also Victorian. Within this area, the free-flying staircase comes straight down in front of the dining room, and then it proceeds on down in this more formal way.

With such a very complex structure it is to be expected that the actual wall surfaces will be complicated, too, as they spiral down and round the stairs. These are areas that look like triangles, enormous lofty walls that reach right up twenty five feet, and then little intimate walls that are just on the galleried part outside the dining room.

From the doorway of the sitting room on the first floor landing you see the galleried walk leading to the lower staircase. Two identical panels are stenciled with young camellia trees.

THE DECORATIVE TREATMENT

The structure of the staircase has been painted a soft yellow. First it was painted a glowing bright yellow, but this proved to be too strong for that part of the staircase that is quite an enclosed area, and so it was given a milky glaze to soften it down and mellow it. It brings a marvelous feeling of sunlight into this extraordinary area.

The staircase itself is by no means without light. There is a long window all up one wall which ends in a rather pretty gothic pointed top, and so light does fall into this space very beauti-fully, and at times, very glowingly and very dramatically. The walls have been painted over their initial coating of white, washed a Mediterranean soft blue to simulate skies on the best of days. Across this beautiful blue which has some green in it as well, we have stenciled a variety of different camellia bushes, some of which reach into the lofty heights of the tallest areas, and some are quite sturdy and just fit snugly into more enclosed parts, and appear to be of more stunted growth. Where they soar up into the ceiling we have flying yellow birds which are probably canaries, but the yellow looks good and goes well with the

OPPOSITE From the third floor one gets a splendid view through the long window of the slate rooftops that ring the harbor of Penzance. The stencils fold around the corners to decorate the narrow walls bordering this window.

TOP The suspended platform between the first and third floor of the staircase provides an ideal position for viewing the stenciled walls.

glowing yellow of the staircase itself. The flowers vary according to their placing on the walls, and because of the nature of stenciling one is able to add to the variety of these shrubs by merely changing the color used. White camellias have strongly dark green leaves; pink camellias have leaves of a paler, yellower green, while the crimson flowers have some mid-way between the two. This change in color, together with the reversing and shortening of stencils, provide us with the necessary natural look I wanted here, quite unlike the more formal tree of life in the sitting room. However, there is an affinity, for at the base of each trunk is a grassy tuft anchoring the bushes to the baseboard.

The more fluid and natural approach here is aided by some languid grasses that help to fill the area between this base and the lower branches. Among these lower branches flutter some fantastic butterflies, larger than life and delightfully colorful.

Underlying the seemingly random placing of the stencils there is a formality, as with the regular placing of a single tree each side of the dining room door. There are three trees falling away down the slope of the stairs on one particular wall, and on the other wall three more matching it. So there is an underlying evenness to the distribution of the trees as indeed there would be in nature.

TOP A close view of a part of the landing wall where two different kinds of camellias merge. The difference is, in fact, only in change of coloring as they are the same stencil.

RIGHT One of a pair of camellias flanking the dining room door on the first floor landing. In the top corner a butterfly dances attendance.

Because of the particular nature of the designs and the height of the hall, we hired a box scaffold so that two or more people would work together at the same height. The stencils we were using needed more than one person to position them. They were made up as whole trees and measured within the region of $6' \times 4'$. In order to make sure that these lay flat against the wall it was necessary to hang them across the surface of the wall from the top. When they were lined up properly, they were pushed gently but firmly onto the surface from the top down so

that they lay flat. To exploit to the full the feeling that one was walking up the stairs through a garden grove, it was at times necessary to bend the branches around the adjoining wall. Tape was placed down the crease in the corner of the wall, and the stencil was positioned over it. At one point, halfway up the very narrow wall that reaches from top to bottom of the very long window, it seemed as though there ought to be some sort of stenciling. This is where this bending round of a branch from one wall onto another was particularly appropriate.

LEFT Three different stencils of birds were cut to occupy this stairway shrubbery; one in flight and the other two to perch among the branches. Canary yellow coloring ensures they are not too camouflaged among the dark leaves.

THE UPSTAIRS HALL

Back at the top of the stairs, if you duck your head and pass through a low arched way, you come into a more intimate area immediately outside the nursery rooms. Obviously, a scheme on such a grand scale as in the rest of the hall would not be appropriate here. A small hall area would feel rather overcrowded with designs of such scale. Here we have used a simpler decorative device to embellish its creamy walls and small doors. On the top panel of each of these three doors is a small branch of box leaves, loosely tied with a turquoise ribbon. A simple leaf alone adorns the walls. This is an easy and most effective way to stencil small areas or rooms such as lavatories, as the exact placing of each leaf is not essential.

Being presented initially with a hall of such scale, it was an ideal opportunity to work on something full-blooded and exotic but without creating an overpowering and claustrophobic feeling. Not only does the window add to the light and airiness, but also the fact that the background is of a painted blue which makes it feel as if the sky is beyond; quite where the surface really begins and ends is, at

times, not very clear and difficult to judge. It is only the darkness of the leaves and flowers that actually feel close as the blueness fades away into the distance.

In principal, I feel that a hallway is an area where you can go in for something more elaborate and demanding because it is not a place where you will spend a lot of time. However it is an area in which to create some impact. It is where first impressions are formed when people first enter a house and is also the place that one descends to in the morning after sleeping. Here one welcomes friends, and so it does seem a chance to display one's personal style clearly and take up a very definite stance. Another point about using more elaborate stencils in a hall is that there is usually a smaller area to cover than any other room and so you could really spend time working into these smaller spaces to produce quite elaborate stenciled effects. Usually most halls are underfurnished compared to other rooms in the house, apart from the odd hall table and a few chairs, and the walls are left clear and bare, and again a grand canvas presents itself on which to lay out your design statements. Maybe these will take the form of an overall design or they could consist of some elaborate frieze or a particular wide decorative banding to surround all the doors that inevitably lead from such areas. On the other hand, it is an ideal place to stencil a floor which can be shown off to great advantage. However, if you are stenciling a hall floor do make sure that you give it plenty of coats of varnish as it is going to get a lot of use.

OPPOSITE A simple motif of slips of box leaves loosely tied with a blue ribbon.

LEFT The small area connecting the main hall with the nursery rooms has a much simpler treatment. Spaced regularly across its creamy surface is a single sprig of box leaves.

THE
DINING ROOM

U PSTAIRS *I have made a second floor room – probably the most extraordinary room of the Old Customs House – into the dining room. Traditionally, in houses where staff was employed, the dining room was located far away from the kitchen, so that everything had to be carried up and down, and high above the street, so that distressful odors and intrusive noise could be avoided. The staff may be gone but in this house the custom still lingers.*

THE ROOM'S PHYSICAL FEATURES

The dining room, with its barrel-shaped ceiling, is situated in the very center of the house in the middle of the second floor. It really is a very secret room indeed, and I think it might have been a private chapel at the time of the Reformation because the ceiling, which is so beautiful, reminds me of a church as it curves gently overhead in a lovely generous sweep. The room is similar in feeling to the nurseries on the very top floor, where the ceilings have a similarly complicated make-up. Here, the same extraordinary ledge changes from being the wall into being the ceiling proper. Under this ledge, the walls fall away in their usual undulating way that I have grown to cherish in this lovely old house.

The dining room is very much an interior room. It has an interior window that looks right onto the main large stairway space – the core of the building. Opposite this is a beautiful

window which is sectioned in three parts – a central part and two side panels, all paned in traditional Georgian fashion.

Outside this window, a very narrow passageway, that is the Old Customs House Lane, runs down beside the house. The room looks straight onto the lofty granite walls of the Regent Hotel opposite, and so you really do get a very secret feeling in the room. It feels incredibly enclosed and womb-like. However, when you are alone in the room, it is in no way threatening. On the contrary, it is the most delightful room to be in – a congenial shape with high walls and an absolutely exceptional ceiling.

My plan to use the eternal vine as a convivial subject for the decoration of the dining room was compounded by the discovery of some superb old stenciling of this subject in the north of Cornwall. This involved the overall display of the vine in two colors with columns and leaves covering the whole surface of the wall.

Though the room appears to be replete with stenciling here, when I finally finished it, I had stenciled the floor with the columns and the ceiling trellis with the vine.

THE STENCIL SCHEME

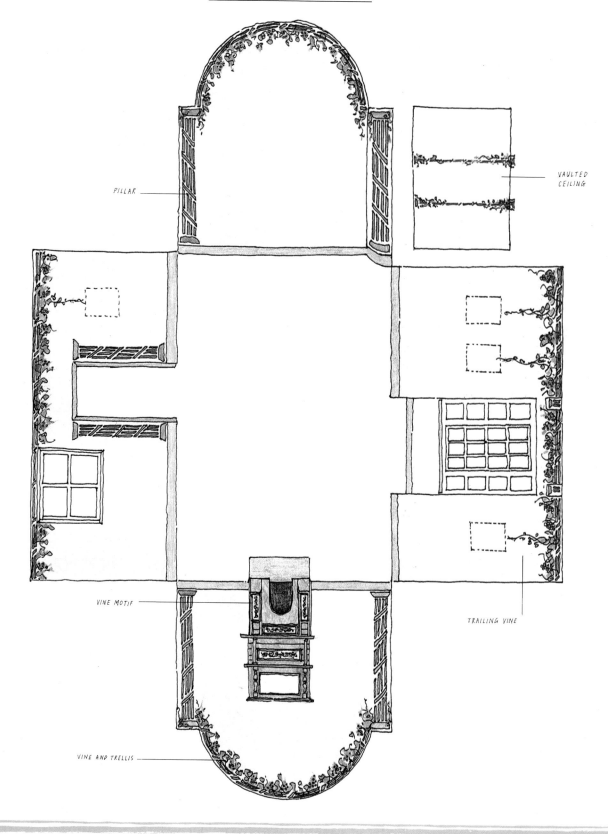

PILLAR

VAULTED CEILING

VINE MOTIF

TRAILING VINE

VINE AND TRELLIS

LEFT The dining room before I started work on it.

BELOW The grapes of the old stencilwork are in alternate bunches of blue and green with black stems and green leaves. Crude columns in a lovely rose color are spaced approximately 15 inches apart and form the structure behind this abundant spread of vines. Part of this elaborate scheme had been carefully uncovered by the painstaking work of the owner of the house; he removed all the water-based paints covering portions of the wall to unveil this gloriously free decoration. Most fortunately it had been carried out in gloss paint, and so the color remains clear and strong.

THE DESIGN CONCEPT

The treatment of the room, as far as the stenciling is concerned, is to produce an effect of a vine-clad bower. Placed firmly onto each corner of the room are tall pillars of glowing limestone quality – and these seem to sturdily support it. They really do give that illusion; they feel as if they are holding the canopy up over the room.

Overhead are the vines with their pale green grapes and very dark green leaves that cling and twine around rods that arch around each end of the room from pillar to pillar. This carries on under the ledge of the ceiling, and the rods form a good formal structure on which the vine is strung out as it would be in a greenhouse or an arbor.

Across the walls, where pictures are hung, there are these straggling twines of vine leaves coming down almost to reach the top of the picture frames – so that you feel that the pictures are hung from the vine instead of being securely attached to the wall behind.

Stretched across the two long walls, this frieze of vine leaves and grapes is broken up intermittently by the strong wooden supports to the main ceiling. Here, another arching device starts to swing across the center of the ceiling and sweeps down to the other side of the room, furthering this feeling of sitting in an arbor.

I suppose it does seem quite Mediterranean; it certainly doesn't feel English. But the surroundings are appropriately congenial and hospitable for a dining room. I think it has a good feeling of theater, and some very enjoyable evenings could take place under such a canopy.

The curves and spirals of the side table's top and base are also reflected in the ladderback chairs' construction.

THE DECORATIVE TREATMENT

The room encompasses an enormous table and I have tried, apart from the stencilwork, to keep the feeling in here uncluttered, clear and sparse, although not quite monastic. I have, however, set a very elaborate table for the photograph on page 56, and so the initial impression is of a far more crowded room than when the table is cleared.

Bearing in mind the Victorian ideal that a dining room should "breathe of comfort and that repose which acts so beneficially upon the digestive organs when they are summoned into active service", I have sought to produce that necessary calming effect by treating the walls very simply. Their surface has been mottled to resemble creamy whitewash. This had been achieved by using an overall rich cream color overlaid by a dabbing of a paler cream. This, in conjunction with what is already an uneven surface, really does promote the most humane and pleasing of textures, ripe for stencilwork.

In order to keep to the theatricality of the room, the window has for curtains a dramatic swag of very dark green cloth stenciled rather grandly in rich gold. This effect is further enriched by the twists of tassels and cords used to fit the curtain to its pole. Beneath the swag hangs a functional shade with a curved edge that is generously stenciled with a crescent of grapes. Like the window it covers, the shade is constructed of three parts – a central panel and two side pieces.

The vine motif occurs all through the room; it is the most adaptable of all

The trailing vine branching off from the main border provides a very effective linking device to the portraits. It almost appears as if they were hanging from the vine rather than on the wall.

plants as it twines and curves in the most agreeable fashion in order to decorate diverse shapes and surfaces. It can be used on almost anything to which you should want to apply a pattern. It is not by chance that vines have been used throughout the ages in just this manner.

At one end of the room is a fireplace; it has some panels that lend themselves very ably to stenciling, and we have again brought the vine into play, increasing its imprint further. The wooden frame of the fireplace has been marbleized, not in an effete manner, but roughly in order to keep to the rustic feeling of this room that displays a total lack of real symmetry. Green china has been used to decorate the two high mantle shelves, as well as on the table.

Hanging from the center ceiling is a simple wooden candelabra. It has a hexagonal wooden structure which holds candles, and is attached to the ceiling by a chain which is wrapped around with the lush dark green cloth stenciled with the gold vine. By the wall, next to the window, stands a cool marble-topped side table laid with dark green coffee cups and some good English cheeses. If you look closely, you will see a vine-covered pitcher. This also helped to influence my design for the decoration. The table's spiraling wooden base has the same feeling as the chairs, rather Moorish. The serpentine curves of its marble top curvingly echo the backs of the chairs and the base of the shade.

The portraits hanging on the wall are not of my relatives but were a lucky find in an antique shop some time ago. I had no particular use for them at the time, but they cost very little and it's quite rare to come across a group of paintings such as these.

I believe they are all members of a Cornish family; the father, in naval dress, hangs on an opposing wall, and I feel the family is very much at home here in this room.

TOP AND BOTTOM I chose the china pieces to echo the room's imagery. In fact, the pitcher was one of the early inspirations for the way the vine motif evolved as a border.

LEFT I finished painting the floor and fireplace after the main photographs of the room were done. The floor was painted greige and I used the columns to create a border pattern that stopped just short of the fireplace.
I applied false marbling on the baseboards around the door and on the fireplace. The vine motif was applied to the panels that were further defined by a soft orange border. The fireplace opening is trompe l'oeil. It was created by painting the requisite shape in matte black over the false marbling of the boarded-in area.

THE TABLECLOTHS AND NAPKINS

On the dining table I have laid a classical white damask cloth over a dark green baize silence cloth. The silence cloth, similar to the draped curtain, is stamped out with the golden vine all around its base.

On top of the damask cloth are damask napkins that have been stenciled with wreaths of vine leaves, and they have been placed around the table to form the table settings. The circular imagery provides an attractive frame for the dinner plates. Of course, on a much smaller tablecloth, this type of stenciled image could work well as a setting for a centerpiece if it was placed in the middle of the cloth. In any event, the napkins do make a very

adaptable format as a table covering if you want to vary the number of places. They can be moved closer or further apart according to the numbers you want to accommodate at your table. Since they are used as a table covering, you would need other plain napkins in addition.

Set around the table are some Spanish weaving chairs. These are painted a good bright canary yellow. Each has the vine imagery decorating its three slats, front and back.

It is always worth stenciling some less obvious areas, like the sides and backs of bits of furniture, so that they are fully decorated. In this way, the job is full-hearted and there is no skimpiness about the way in which the decorative treatment has been carried out.

Rather than decorate the large expanse of tablecloth, I've restricted the painting to individual napkins. Therefore, should the unthinkable have happened – some mishap with the painting – I've limited the damage to single squares of damask.

MAKING A WINDOW SHADE

Stenciling is the ideal decoration for a window shade, especially the simplest roller type, but it can be used to decorate Roman shades or fabric that is to be made up into more elaborate shapes.

You can either use a ready-made single color shade, or easily create a more specialized shape out of plain canvas. Here, I could have used a simpler rectangular-shaped shade, but by cutting the material with a curved edge, the finished shade is much more effective. The stenciling is easy, the only difficult part is the shade's construction.

To create this particular shape, I joined to the central panel, two similarly cut side pieces. I used a wide hem all around and on the joins to give more substance to the blind so that it would hang better. The paper pattern I created to cut out the material, I also used for cutting the pieces of stencil card. These had to be joined similarly to the material. Then I sprayed a crescent of grapes onto the bottom of the shade. To complete the look, I painted the vine stencil, using bright gold, onto the dark green curtain material.

1 *I joined three pieces of plain canvas and reinforced the hem and joins with double stitching so it would hang better.*

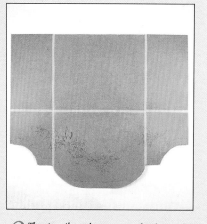

2 *The stencil card was cut to the shape of the finished shade, accurately copying its curved edge.*

3 *I then drew the vine and grapes in a crescent shape onto the stencil card.*

4 *The cut-out stencil was laid upon the canvas and then the paint was applied.*

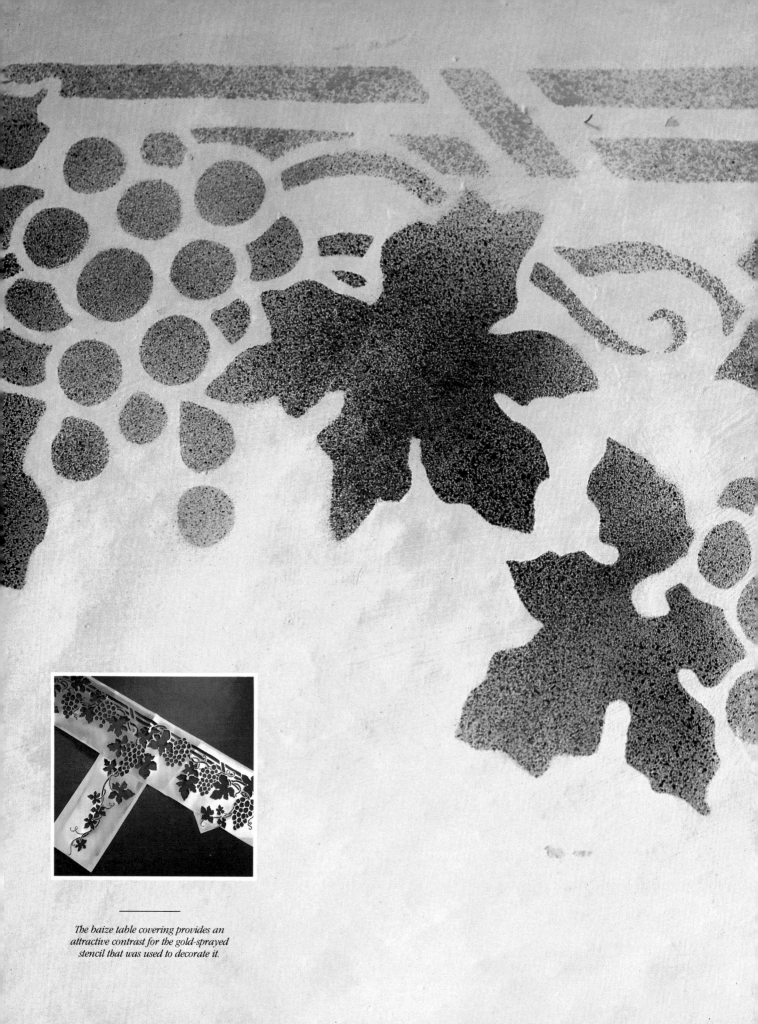

The baize table covering provides an
attractive contrast for the gold-sprayed
stencil that was used to decorate it.

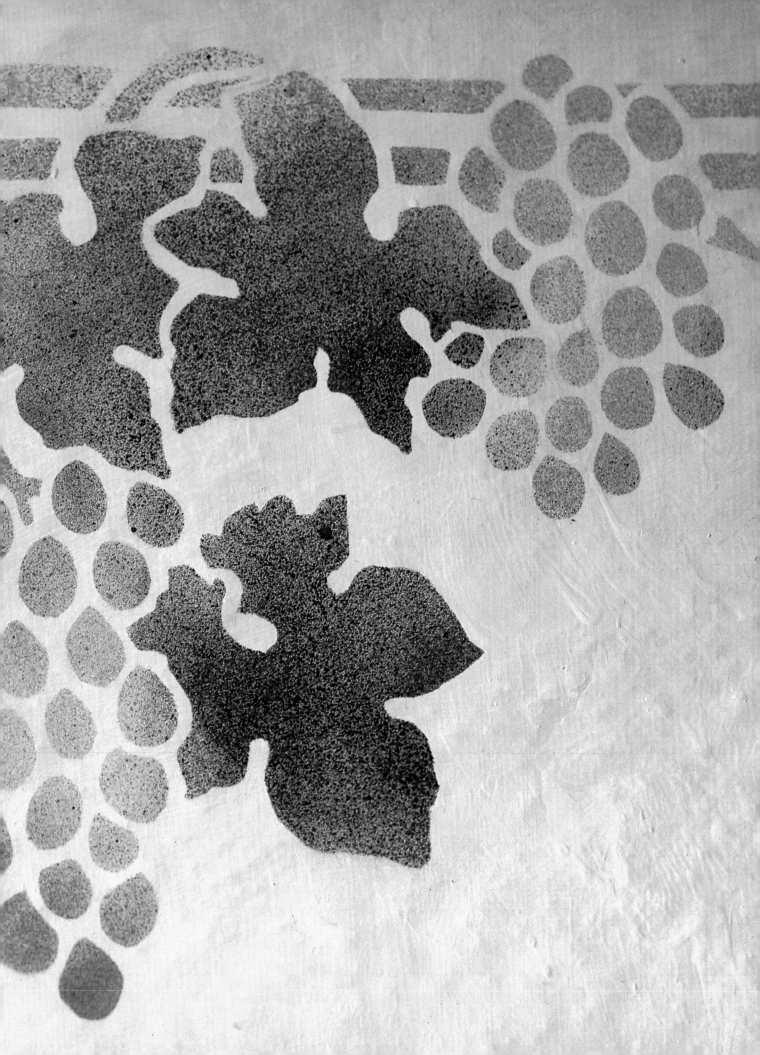

CREATING COLUMNS

Only one stencil was used for the columns. If, as in the pillar below right, there is a greater than normal area left between the two diagonals, you simply spray up to the bottom diagonal, move the stencil and finish it off. The discrepancy won't be noticed.

1 In order to achieve the mottled texture of the columns, a card guard that has been intricately trimmed, was placed between the stencil and the spray paint.

2 I hung the stencil from the bottom and sprayed the base of the column just short of its top portion.

3 I then moved the stencil up to the required height in order to complete the top part of the column.

4 Here, I have to move the stencil up and mask the diagonal to cover the unpainted area with sufficient vertical stripes.

STENCILING INTO AN
AWKWARD CORNER

Stenciling is so adaptable it can be used to decorate successfully even the most difficult areas.

1 Where the walls meet the curve of the ceiling, a complicated corner cannot be left unpainted.

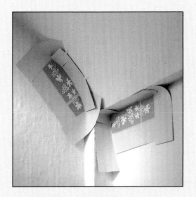

2 Strips of stenciled frieze can be set into the corners of the wall and ceiling. Here, they are masked off ready to spray.

3 When the corners are sprayed, additional stencils are added to form a pillar with cascading leaves.

THE
SITTING ROOM

SITUATED ON *the first floor so that its fine Georgian windows overlook the street, the Sitting Room of the Old Customs House is a very light room – fine, large and shallow. In the morning, when the pale sunlight begins to come in through the windows, the room feels fresh and lively, while on dull afternoons it is a warming and cheerful place to be, because the color inside the room obliterates the grayness outside. On sunny evenings it is simply radiant, while later, by fire and lamplight, it does have the most glamorous feeling of all.*

THE DESIGN CONCEPT

Rather than work against the shallow feeling of the room, which I found very pleasing, I have further emphasized it by concentrating the decoration on the upper portion of the walls.

I chose a trompe l'oeil effect of panels – strong, central images contained within a sharply-defined but small stenciled border. The ceiling already has an impressive and elaborate cornice, so that the paneling doesn't seem inappropriate, meeting as it does this well-rounded and undulating cornice in order to link it with the ceiling. To divide off the lower portion of the room, I have put in a false dado line which gives the impression of its being a much finer room than, in fact, it is.

On summer days, when there is no need for a fire we have a further building-up of pattern as a decorated fireboard is fixed in front of the grate. This fireboard is covered in velvet and stenciled with a variety of evocative images, the sort which you can imagine a child sitting and looking at intensely as they imprint themselves on the memory. These very disparate images are of birds eating cherries, strangely cumbersome butterflies, little snails creeping along the ground between a scattering of millefleurs and, in one corner, an outsized tulip. In the period in which this sort of imagery was current, tulips were a great curiosity as I believe they were at that time newly imported, and so scarce a commodity that much-coveted bulbs fetched a great price.

I do feel that the stenciling has enhanced the intrinsic architecture of the Sitting Room while not diverting from its faults. The imposed panels break up the surface of the walls, giving them a formal proportioning they did not have. The largest panels, centrally placed on the walls, have narrow panels on either side.

The decoration ensures that this is the ideal setting in which to entertain friends or to relax on one's own, reading or dreaming.

The mirror hung between the windows demonstrates that the irreverent placing of objects over stencilwork is perfectly acceptable, only adding to the overall richness.

THE DECORATIVE
TREATMENT

Within the panels I have devised a
quite naive interpretation of the tree
of life – an old design taken from ancient Indian textiles, I am not alone in
finding such imagery extremely ap-
proriate for a sitting room or a living
room, as many other designers have
found this motif endlessly fascinating
as it curls and twines into its convoluted
shape. It contains the most surprising
variety of flowers and fruits, none of
which could ever possibly grow on a
single tree in real life. The tree as I've

cut it grows most vigorously out of a
hump made up of small hillocks which
are very fertile, producing many little
flowers of, again, extraordinary variety,
quite unidentifiable in botanical terms.
The colors are strong and clear, and I
feel evolve well with all the changing
moods of the room.

For the imagery on the fireboard I
drew from an old form of needlework
called stumpwork. One finds it in
many of the National Trust houses in
this western corner of England, particularly at Trerice where they have an
extremely fine collection of stumpwork pictures.

*My tree of life's convoluted
shapes are eternally fascinating.*

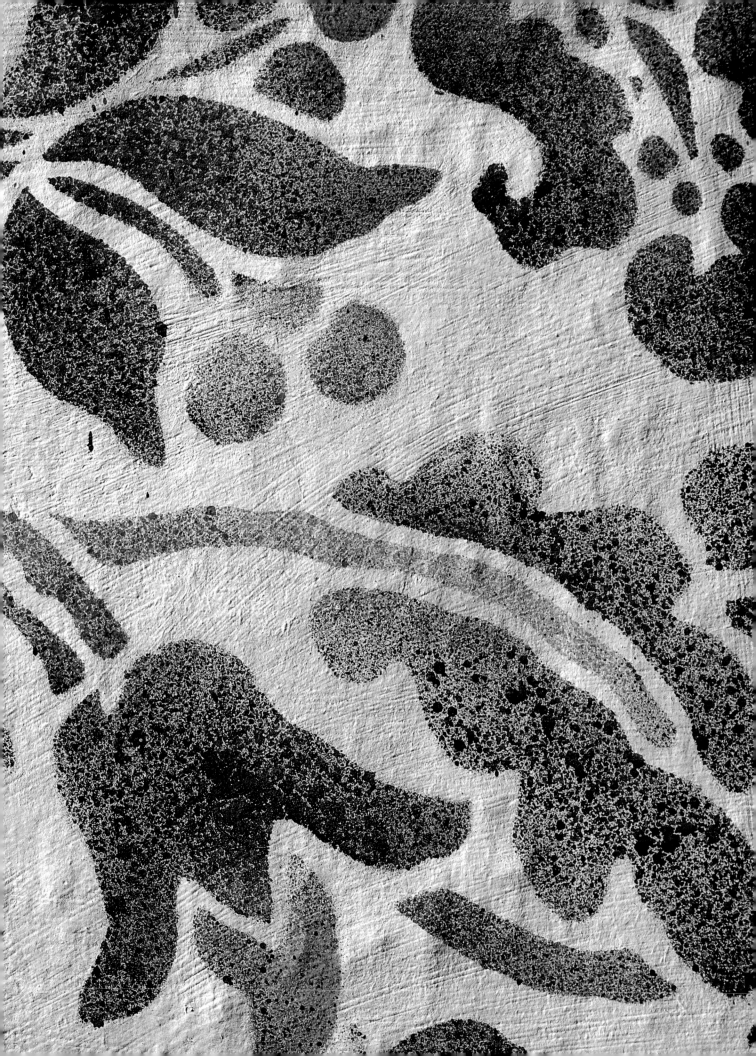

Above the broad mantlepiece, which is made of a rather beautiful gray marble, the space needed to be broken up because it was long and didn't have the height that one would need to place a single panel, so I broke it up with three little narrow panels, which make good foils for the candlesticks, and a central panel. This works well with the construction of the fireplace underneath it.

The bergère sofa and chairs in the room are reproductions of no special antique value but were transformed by the addition of some paint and plain upholstery. I used a pale pearly gray and, where the carving and indentations occurred on the bases and edges of the furniture, the color built up and emphasized their shapes.

Lattice upon canework gives a look that is very attractive and lightens the entire appearance of the furniture. It was achieved by painting across the whole of the canework with gray and then, when this was dry, applying tape diagonally in both directions leaving a 4-inch gap. Great care was taken to make sure that tape was applied in exactly the same areas both sides of the cane. A gold and beige color was sprayed onto the areas not protected by the tapes. The upholstered areas had to be very carefully marked off in order to safeguard against any over-spilling of spray onto these vulnerable areas.

The whole feeling of the furniture is light and airy, enhancing the feeling of a sunny seaside sitting room.

TOP Three panels were needed above the fireplace to prevent the central panel from being ungainly and too broad.

RIGHT A small stool of Indian inspiration has its top decorated with a beaming sun, while the rest of the surfaces are covered with stars.

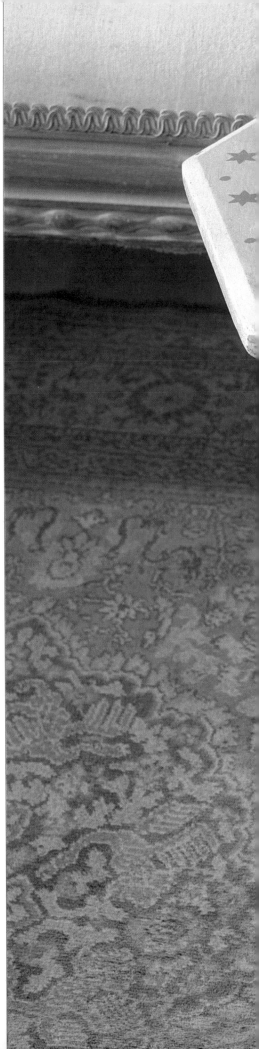

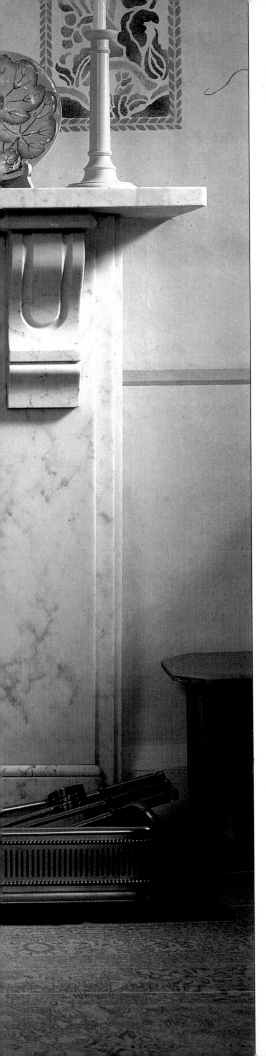

In the warmer weather when an open fire is not required, a fireboard can make an otherwise unattractive area look inviting. Originally, I had planned to stencil a board of painted plasterboard but the finished effect was so flat, I covered the board in velvet instead. This produced a much softer finish that was

more in harmony with the rest of the room.

I based the images on those found in a form of padded embroidery known as stumpwork, examples of which can be found in many stately homes around Cornwall. The design, which at first glance appears to be an overall pattern, is really a collection of disparate images.

1 The fireboard's stencil is a good example of how work progresses. Here, I've begun to sketch in the last major element.

2 Now I've defined the areas to be cut out with cross-hatching – both in the plant and butterfly motifs and in the border.

3 The stencil is now completely cut out and ready for spraying. You can see how in quite a few places, notably the sun, I've altered the final design in the cutting.

4 On a large stencil such as this one where I've joined two pieces of card together, its important to use only one piece of tape each side or it would be too difficult to cut out the shapes.

THE STENCILED LAMPSHADES

It's easy to create lampshades out of strong pieces of card. I created a template that was used to paint the tops and bottoms here, and to cut out the smaller, undecorated candle shades on the desk and mantlepiece.

I've stenciled these shades using the same stumpwork imagery as found on the fireboard. They do look very lively when they are lit up at night, when every speck of paint shows up well from the light below.

They have a particular quality that you don't get from stencilwork at any other time. Perhaps one might get it from a stenciled shade when the light is shining from behind, but on this card, as the design is printed on it with these minute specks of paint, they look very appealing close up. It is very important that images have a good fine quality when one is near them. As with the cushions, the colored detailing should bear close inspection.

I've also stenciled the lamp base using other images taken from the fireboard. The lamps, which are commercially produced to have an eggshell lacquer finish, provide an attractive setting for the stencilwork. The crackling surface offsets it well.

TOP Lampshades make ideal subjects for stenciling; when the lamp is on, every particle of color is brought out with the light.

RIGHT Elements of the imagery from the stenciled fireboard are used to decorate individual cushions; their edges are treated to the same piquéd finish as the curtains. The Cornish camellias bank up exotically to provide more color.

THE CUSHIONS AND CURTAINS

Both the cushions and the curtains were made from a polyester and cotton chintz material, and both have lacey, piquéd edges.

To form these frills, the edges of the chintz were cut with pinking shears and punched with holes using different-sized paper hole punchers.

The cushion frills were then lightly sprayed in green or peach. The cushion cloth had to be stenciled separately, and there are images front and back. Again, the same stenciled designs as appeared on the fireboard have been used here as individual motifs. The stumpwork motifs, because of their variety and scale and size, are particularly good for cushions because you can fill in little corners with the odd moth, flower, or insect.

The curtains, though grand in appearance, are of quite simple construction. They are straight lengths of material with a gathered heading and a frill down their meeting edges, and are caught by generous fabric tie-backs. I padded the top of the curtains with some cotton to make them stand proud and give them body. Done this way, the heading helps to disguise any unevenness in the ceiling.

For extra interest, I stenciled the border of the window shade in keeping with the rest of the room's coloring and imagery. This is quite a simple, though effective, technique as only a small amount of spraying is required to produce an effect with a fair amount of impact.

Both the curtains and cushions were trimmed with a decorative lace made of chintz cut with pinking shears and punched with holes. Different-sized punchers were used to produce the correct scale.

THE PAINTED DESK

The desk, which I placed between the windows, was a rather undistinguished item of furniture before I began working on it. It is, however, the kind of piece that gains a great deal from being decorated in a thorough fashion.

The desk was originally cloaked in a dreary gravy brown color that had no merit whatsoever. However, it did have the handsome ball and claw feet and the drop flap with the very pretty little pocket-like shelves set into its interior. Its construction was basically interesting and it had the potential of being a very attractive piece.

By painting it a dull Indian red, the sort of red the Chinese used to lacquer boxes, furniture and screens, and by applying gold stenciling, I have managed to transform it. Afterwards, a coat of gloss varnish, something I seldom use, was applied to it to give it a stronger connotation of having some affinity with China. Once it was varnished, it was polished many times with some very good furniture wax, and this gave the initial slightly tacky gleam of the varnish a deeper, denser, more revolved sheen.

I have given it a lovely dark green interior, the color of a billiard table. Over this I have used a little tiny flower stencil that often occurs on stumpwork backgrounds. Here it is sprigged across the dark green paintwork as an infill so that when one is sitting at the desk writing a letter, there are these pleasing little flowers peeping out behind the objects on the desk – a small luxury.

When painting the interior of this desk, we carefully left the rather pretty coloring of the wood at the front edge of these shelf units, and painted only the interiors of these pockets and the main flat areas. We were also very careful to avoid painting over the leatherette set into the flap-down shelf that is the writing area.

The green interior also makes a vibrant contrast with the rich Indian

red of the external casework. Over this, in gold, I have stenciled some of the fireboard imagery, as well as incorporating the border from the tree of life panels.

The handles on the drawers have also been transformed, set as they now are with the little stenciled flowers on the new rich coloring. Like Cinderella, they now look far more elegant than when they hung dully over the rather dreary brown wood.

The candle shades on the desk were

made from pieces of stencil card; the same template used to paint the lamp shades was used here as a guide to trim their bottoms.

The beautiful old mirror above the desk shows how suitable it is to hang articles over stencil work and not feel this to be taboo. The mirror sits most happily on this enriched surface and somehow intensifies the texture of the stenciling by its very interruption.

The liberal use of stenciling, both inside and out, has transformed what was originally a fairly ordinary piece of reproduction furniture into something quite eye-catching.

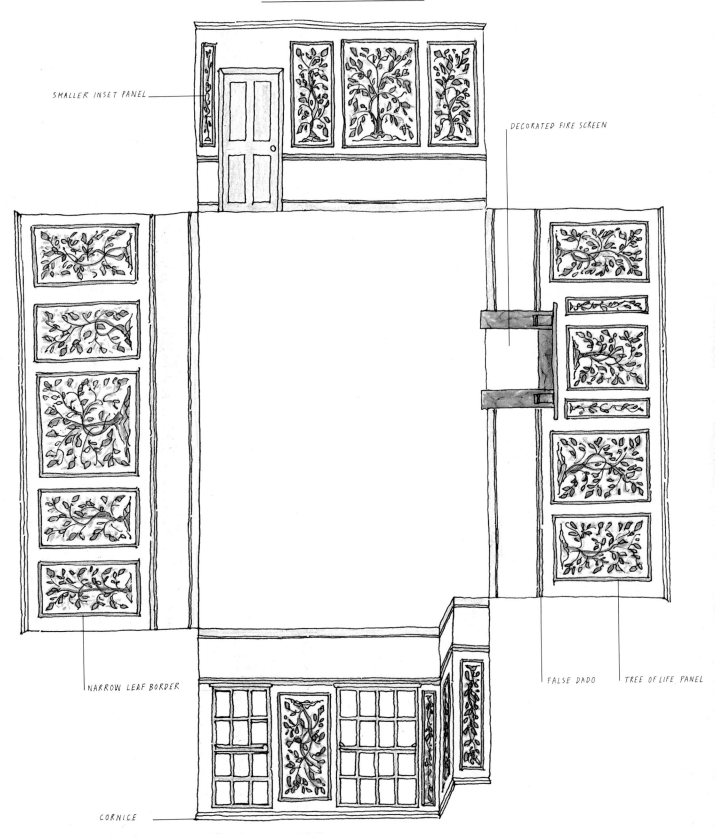

SMALLER INSET PANEL

DECORATED FIRE SCREEN

NARROW LEAF BORDER

FALSE DADO

TREE OF LIFE PANEL

CORNICE

THE
PAISLEY BEDROOM

O *N THE FIRST floor of the Old Customs House, at the end of a long high passage, is the Paisley Bedroom. A small room with a tall ceiling, it is lit from one small sash window and a thin long window inserted into the corner fabric of the house at a most extraordinary angle. The room was naturally dark and we added to its intimacy by keeping the colors rich and strong as well. It is a cozy room in the winter, with its warm textures and colors.*

THE ROOM'S PHYSICAL FEATURES

When we first started working on the room, the long window was, in fact, inside a cupboard. But, as the room was dimly lit by the one window, it seemed a good idea to open the window out to include this particular area of cupboard and bring it in as part of the room as a whole. The window has a wide, triangular windowsill and altogether gives an almost medieval feel to the room with its slanting slit. Above the door, which is very small and low, is another window that lets light into the passage. I have chosen to actually give all these windows a slightly gothic look by putting curved and pointed cornices above them. These cornices tie in with the hangings of the sleigh bed which is the main feature of the room.

A powerful illusion is created in the room by the stenciled floor. The natural floor undulates considerably and in order to cope with this problem of

extreme levels it seemed a good idea to create further differences by putting in a floor that gives the impression of dropped panels. This has the trompe-l'oeil effect of not quite knowing where the actual surface of the floor is, because the center of each boxed panel seems to have a further depth to it. Within the center of this panel sits a geometric star. The look that we were seeking was one of marquetry and the feeling of the whole floor is one of richness. Each of the different sections that makes up the floor has been grained to look like a particular wood, and so we have the walnut and ebony stars in the center, sitting on a base of pale yew. To the two sides of this there are rich mahogany bindings, and to the other two sides there is something that might be walnut or even chestnut. Around it is a border of a good strong slab of chestnut. So the illusion works in two ways. It works to break up the feeling of where the actual surface of this floor is, and there is an illusion of wood when in fact it is made up from paint on hardboard. Very careful

The sleigh bed dominates the small bedroom with its stenciled cushions and paisley patterned curtains. Other, more sparsely patterned curtains hang from the walls. The painted floor simulates the mahogany of the bed frame.

preparation was put into the laying of the hardboard. Every square is, in fact, a separate piece and the border round the edges formed by a solid border mitered at the corners. This construction furthers the illusion that the floor is made out of blocks of wood intricately pieced together.

The basic wall paint for this room is a rich deep ocher and brushed across with a light covering of pale latex paint to give the surface of the walls a bloom. This wall color only appears between and above the curtains and, breaking

with my general rule of always painting ceilings white, we painted the ceiling of this room also with the ocher to give a more enclosed tented feeling. However, the paleness of the velvet with its figuration of palms is designed to counteract too stifling a feeling on a summer's night. The bareness of the floor, which is belied by its rich appearance, is another cooling feature. In the last varnish coat I added a small amount of grayish-white paint that produced an aging patina and made it more ornate. It might well be that in the winter a Persian rug could be added to give this room an even more cozy feeling.

THE BED TREATMENT

Against the back wall above the bed is a scaled-up version of the gothic cornice. This heads the curtains which fall to each side and swoop over the two ends of the bed. The bed itself is covered with plain stone-colored velvet and is strewn with cushions covered with the same fabric in a variety of colors – scarlet, Prussian blue and eau de nil. These are colors which are picked up in the stenciled paisley design printed on the canopy. Traditional paisley designs employ many borders to build up the richness associated with its highly ornamental form of surface design. The design takes the form of a twisting twining palm tree that meanders across the surface of the cloth.

Framing this design at the edges, the top and the bottom of these curtains, there is a border of a small scale pattern of flowers and broken stems that form little nodules along each side. Interspersed within the area between these palm-like forms are repeated small motifs of broken paisley-like leaves.

The bed also has some splendid scarlet bolsters that seem to be *de rigueur* for this kind of bed. The format for the stenciled covering of the cushions is for them to look rather extravagant and voluptuous, covered in velvet and then tied over with little patterned jackets that knot and bow in different ways on each cushion – sometimes at the corners, sometimes across the middle. Even the bolsters are wrapped around with an extra layer, also patterned with the paisley design.

OPPOSITE It is difficult to visualize the scale of the main stencil in this picture. It measures 36" × 76" and spreads across the whole inner width of the fabric so it can be stenciled all at once. Border stencils are then added to each side.

LEFT The stenciled pattern, in muted colors, sits well on the bloom of the parchment-colored cloth.

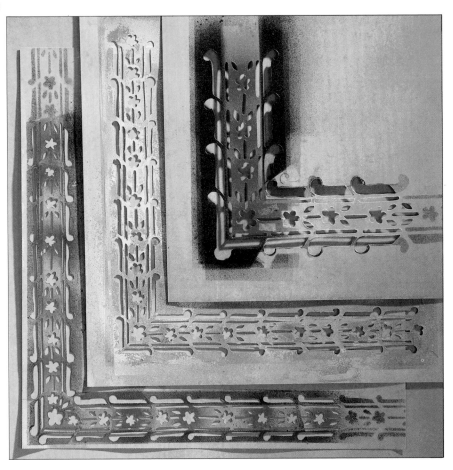

THE WALL PANELS

In addition to the bed, the main walls of the room are hung with the paisleyed velvet. The hangings form cloth panels over the walls; the centers of the panels are left clear except for the odd leaf so we have the elaborate paisley border mainly marking out their edges. These hang loosely from the poles on wooden rings about five inches down from the ceiling and give a rich and voluptuous look. This is at the same time careless and informal.

The elaborate pattern-work is built up with three borders: the small outer border with the simple scalloped flower in the center, then a more typical meandering paisley leaf edged with small chevrons, and then the larger scale of the palm design which fills in the center of the panels after

that. The change of scale is also typical of paisley. These borders in themselves have been built up with bands of different designs within themselves. Between these there is further filling in with the element of the little spotted single leaf.

Among the furniture of the room there is a chest of drawers with a pair of lamps constructed from old banister knobs. These already had a coating of rich syrupy varnish, and all that seemed necessary in the way of finish was to imitate that rich varnish and build up the chestnut varnish in layers on to the elaborate bases. I was then able to apply my stencils on top of this, after which I applied yet another coat of treacly varnish to the whole. This gave them the necessary unified look.

LEFT The stenciled lampshades look particularly attractive when lit up at night, each particle of paint is visible and bright.

TOP A build-up of the stencil borders used to create the complex paisley designs.

THE STENCIL SCHEME

One of the most effective uses of stenciling in the house has been on the floors. Both the Paisley Bedroom and the Parlor (see p.34) are small rooms that benefit enormously from the illusion of space created by painted floors. The effect of the marquetry blocks used here, and the tiled squares of the Parlor, is to visually enlarge both rooms to a remarkable degree. Such a look can be successfully applied to almost any space.

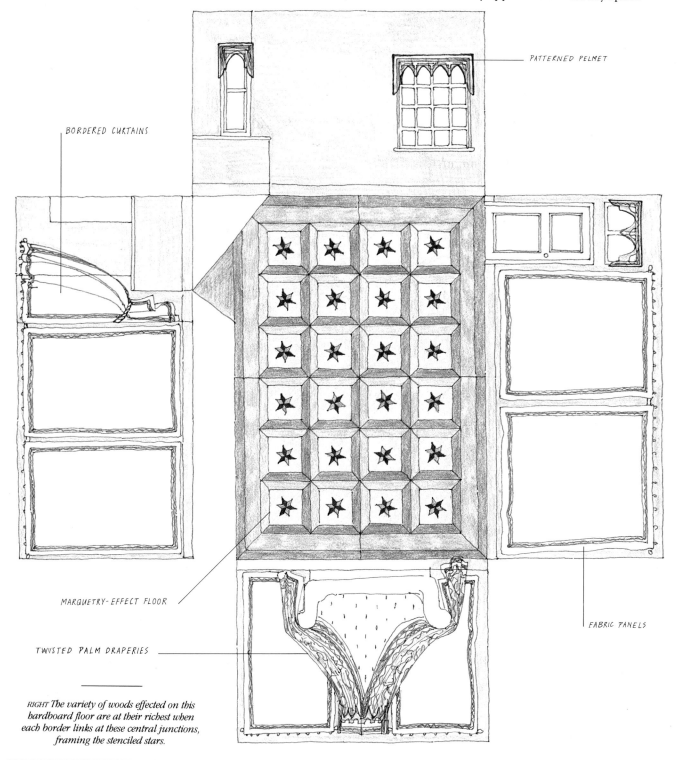

PATTERNED PELMET

BORDERED CURTAINS

MARQUETRY-EFFECT FLOOR

TWISTED PALM DRAPERIES

FABRIC PANELS

RIGHT The variety of woods effected on this hardboard floor are at their richest when each border links at these central junctions, framing the stenciled stars.

THE DECORATIVE
CORNICES

Each of the four cornices made for this room had to be made in a different size and proportion. To start with we have one for the tall narrow window. This has a single arch cut into it. We have the main window cornice which, in order to achieve a gothic effect, has four dags cut out to coincide with the division of the panes of the window. Above the door we have a window with double panes, and so, correspondingly, we have the two arches cut into that. While high up above the bed we have the cornice reaching

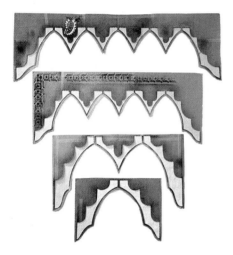

right around two sides of the simple triangular frame. This folds in the center and here we have five arches – the central arch on the fold and two each side. At the two ends of this cornice we have a further curve added at the base as the cloth fits back snugly against the wall.

In order to ensure these cornices fit their respective windows we simply put a piece of stencil card across the windows, marked it to fit the outside of the frame and further allowed two inches extra. The next stage was to draw in the curves that were required. We then used these as templates to cut out the velvet again with an extra inch allowed all around for the seams. Once we had cut the cornices from the stenciled shape we were then able to

use those templates and cut the stencil patterns into them; this was a very economical procedure. We knew that the design that was cut into those shapes would fit exactly onto the velvet and we knew that they would also fit the corresponding windows.

Supporting the bed cornice is a very simple wooden triangular structure one side of which lies flat against the wall. The cornice was fixed to this wooden structure with sticky-backed Velcro. We also used strips of Velcro to attach the other cornice snugly straight onto the surface of the walls around the windows. This meant we didn't have to get involved with constructing elaborate box-like fittings here which would have seemed too elaborate for such humble windows. One enters the room close by the window, and such a protruding structure would have been unwelcome.

Because the velvet that we used in this room was very close-cropped (in fact the trade call this particular cloth suede rather than velvet, its pile is so short) no particular problems were presented at all in stenciling on it. It is unlikely that in working on velvet with a denser pile, any further problem would present itself. It is only when working on something like terry cloth that the image would be seriously interrupted. Stenciling on terry cloth can be seen in the bathroom on both the mat and the towels.

opposite The top three of these stencil templates were made for the different sized windows of this Paisley Bedroom. The fourth cornice was made to cover two sides of the triangular shape fixed about the bed that serves to hide the tops of the curtains.

LEFT The narrow window in the corner of the room has an individually devised cornice specially made to fit it closely. By this fairly simple device, a plain window can be turned into something much more exotic.

THE
BATHROOM

T O ACCOMPANY *the Paisley Bedroom, we have a bathroom painted in an oriental green. It has a finely boned sash window and the usual wobbly, undulating walls. However, the feeling in this room, while aligning itself with the bedroom, is slightly different and does indulge in an overtly tropical look.*

THE DECORATIVE
TREATMENT

During the process of stenciling this room the proportions of it changed like a squeezy box. As we put the main frieze, a twisted cloth of striped jade, around the top of the wall the room became shallow. When we next applied the stripes of the paisley border previously used in the bedroom, this time just in ochers and soft oatmeal tinting, the room again became lofty. This striping stretched from the bottom of the baseboard right up to the frieze. This was another very interesting phenomenon which I enjoyed enormously: playing with space. In between the stripes of the paisley border we placed the single leaf motif to dot the walls and give it the right sort of paisley feel that the accompanying bedroom had. The aim in decorating the bathroom was to create a furnished look, treating the utilitarian objects of bathtub, sink and toilet as furniture and painting them as such. But I altered the feel somewhat by introducing a tropical element. On the

painted linen press which houses all the towels, I have stenciled into the panels a very straight edition of the palm, this time with fruit and a twisted, clinging vine winding up its trunk.

When you open the cupboard, there are three shelves for towels, and along the edges of each shelf there is a nice broad area on which we have stenciled the same, but smaller scale, design that has been used throughout the room. It has been stenciled in a much more monochromatic way, in that you can only just see that it is slightly colored with soft ocher and a pink for the flower. The inside of the cupboard has also been painted with this wonderful wild Mediterranean green.

The floor has bare painted boards which are pale in color which gives a spartan look to that area, as an antidote to the highly decorative surfaces elsewhere in the room. In the center of the ceiling we have stenciled a decorative ceiling medallion around a very ordinary light fixture and this is carried out in the muted colors that are used in the room – that is the jade green, ocher and a deeper blue.

Soft gray floor boards and a muslin screen temper the brilliance of the striped sea green walls and the grandeur of the marbled surfaces. The wreath of leaves repeated on the bathtub also adds pattern to the bath mats. The chair beside the bath has ribbony designs imprinted on its two back bars.

The festoon blind is made of eau de nil moire taffeta that is all but the same color as the walls, edged with a beautiful hand-made lace, in beige. Close in to the window, muslin is stretched across to form a transparent shade, its edges broadly bound in the eau de nil moire taffeta and with the single leaf stenciled across it.

To echo the Paisley Bedroom which this bathroom adjoins, the simplest outer border design was used to plainly stripe its walls. However the coloring was completely different – we merely used two different tones of gold and yellow ocher, but in order to break up its design slightly, we highlighted it with a stoney beige color. Instead of using the blue and scarlet on the small unit leaf, as we had in the adjoining Paisley Room, this time we used ocher gold with the deeper blue marking the seed-like shape in the center of the leaf.

The introduction of marbling has turned this plain little bathroom into something more luxurious and Italian. It seemed really extravagant to use this already contrived surface as a format upon which to stencil. One had to be fairly sure that it was going to be effective enough to take the risk. The effectiveness of the stenciling over the marbling was achieved by using interrelated colors; the same browny reds used in the marbling are also on the leaves, giving them a slightly autumnal appearance.

Painting on the cupboard was more straightforward. The door panels were left a flat stone color while the rest of the casing was also marbled. The illusion that the wooden toilet seat is made of marble is so complete that one expects the lid to be quite heavy when lifting it.

Before we started to work on the bathroom it was one of the those lofty bathrooms with just the basic bathtub, toilet, sink and little else; a very functional room, but not a room to linger in on a wintery morning.

The walls were in a poor condition and they had a scattering of tiles above the sink and bathtub. It also had a rather dire erupting wall to the left as one entered the room. There were a few damp patches on the ceiling that spoke of the same chilled days when pipes had burst. In general, it was difficult to realize at this stage how intrinsically elegant the room was, particularly the window. A plain, good square room with a small door opening diagonally across one corner, and as with all these rooms, it presented a most inviting challenge.

LEFT Within the deep window recess is a Chinese silk embroidery "hanging" from a golden stenciled bow. The muslin curtain at the window is stenciled with a leaf.

TOP Some of the stencil elements used to create the patterns in the bathroom.

103

THE STENCIL SCHEME

The bathroom, before being decorated, was not a welcoming place in which to contemplate spending any time. My somewhat opulent design scheme supplied the missing warmth and intimacy. The exotic border design of twisted cloth, which knots all around the top of the walls at regular intervals, made the proportions seem more manageable and cozy. Paisley stripes, used to provide a link to the adjoining bedroom, also stretched the room out again. By the time I finished, what was probably the house's least attractive room, was fit for royalty.

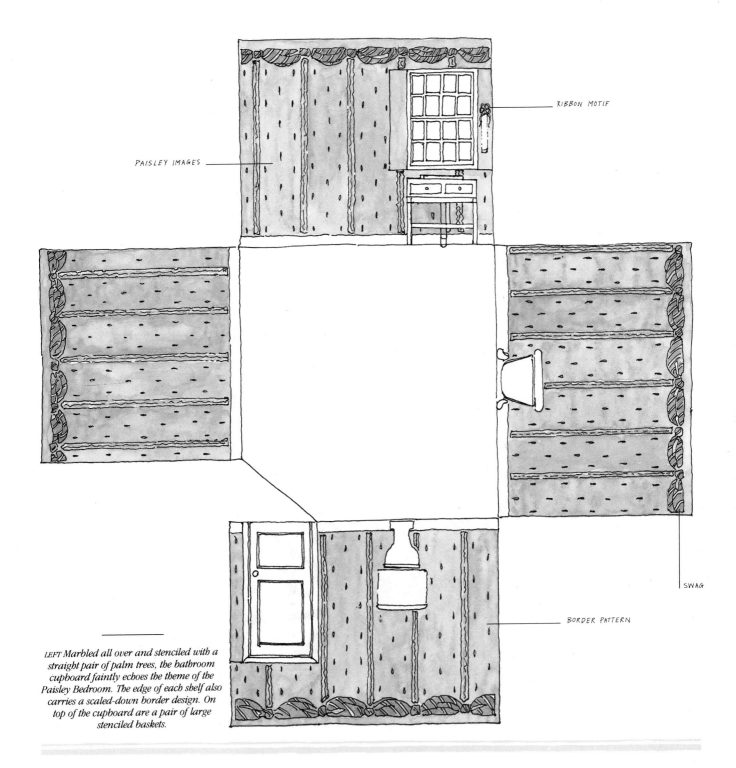

RIBBON MOTIF

PAISLEY IMAGES

SWAG

BORDER PATTERN

LEFT Marbled all over and stenciled with a straight pair of palm trees, the bathroom cupboard faintly echoes the theme of the Paisley Bedroom. The edge of each shelf also carries a scaled-down border design. On top of the cupboard are a pair of large stenciled baskets.

THE FIXTURES AND
FURNISHINGS

The bath, which had looked so forlorn in the original bathroom, has now been transformed into a bath fit for an emperor, or at least the person who sleeps in the Empire bed in the adjoining room. First we renovated the interior surface which had some ugly marks, with the aid of a pack of reconditioning paints from a hardware store. This was a surprisingly simple task. Then the exterior under the curving lip of the bath was marbled by first daubing it a honey beige color. Across this it was finely streaked with meandering lines of rich earth brown and softer golden colors. The marbling gives a good look to the bathroom and feels like a suitable hard surface that just works well, particularly on the side of the bath where the marbled effect has been applied all over the outer part of its great belly. This has been stenciled over with a vaguely imperial wreath of leaves which ties up with the Empire look of the bed in the next room. The same treatment has been given to the toilet seat. In fact, it looks as if it might be very heavy, but there is a warm wooden seat under the coating of marble, with a little motif of leaves and berries on the center of the lid.

Hanging over the edge of the bath is a bathmat that has been stenciled. You can see how the pile of the terry cloth has slightly disrupted the edge of the stenciled image but in no way diminished its general effectiveness. It has a similar sort of quality as stenciling on basket work, in that the edges can be disrupted but the power of the image remains strong.

The bathroom chair has been stripped and the wood has been softened with an overall thin layer of white latex. It has peach-colored leaves stenciled onto the back bars, and a peach flower in the center of a little rosette. There is also a towel rack which has

been painted a wishy-washy gray as has the reeded screen behind the bathtub which has stenciled muslin curtains. A small leaf design has been stenciled onto these muslin curtains which have been made to fit each panel and tied to the screen with pinked taffeta ribbons.

The sink is set into a washstand so that it feels more like a piece of furniture than a bit of plumbing, and the underneath shelf is very useful for baskets of different things one needs in a bathroom like soaps and lotions, brushes and washcloths. In order to keep the furnished look to the room I have also used a small swivel mirror on the deep window ledge. This has also been softened down to a pearly gray color. The candlesticks and posies all add more to the furnished look that I was wanting and to continue with this theme, beside the bathtub there is a small stenciled table holding things like a soap dish, etc.

The imagery on the basketwork of the large bins on the top of the linen cupboard are of the same leaves and berries as the toilet seat, just sprayed across their surface. Surprisingly, the complete look of these images is in no way diminished by the broken nature of this surface.

TOP Before I began work, the bathroom, with its nicely bellied bathtub, presented a challenge to relish, a canvas to paint up.

LEFT The painted color most dominant in this bathroom is a brilliant Caribbean color mid-way between eau de nil and turquoise. The muslin screen around the top of the bathtub provides a feeling of intimacy in this tall room.

STENCILING A SWAG

Sometimes two (or more) stencils have to be used together to provide a more elaborate effect. One is cut fairly broadly and leaves a simple painted area. The other is more finely detailed and provides the final image with all its refinements.

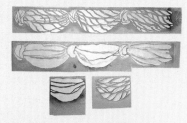

The stencils used to create the illusion of raised awning for the bathroom frieze. The short sections were used to bridge gaps left at the end of each wall.

The first plain outline of the cloth sprayed in golden beige onto the green walls.

The same area overprinted with the striped stencil, this time in a strong green, with the beige showing through.

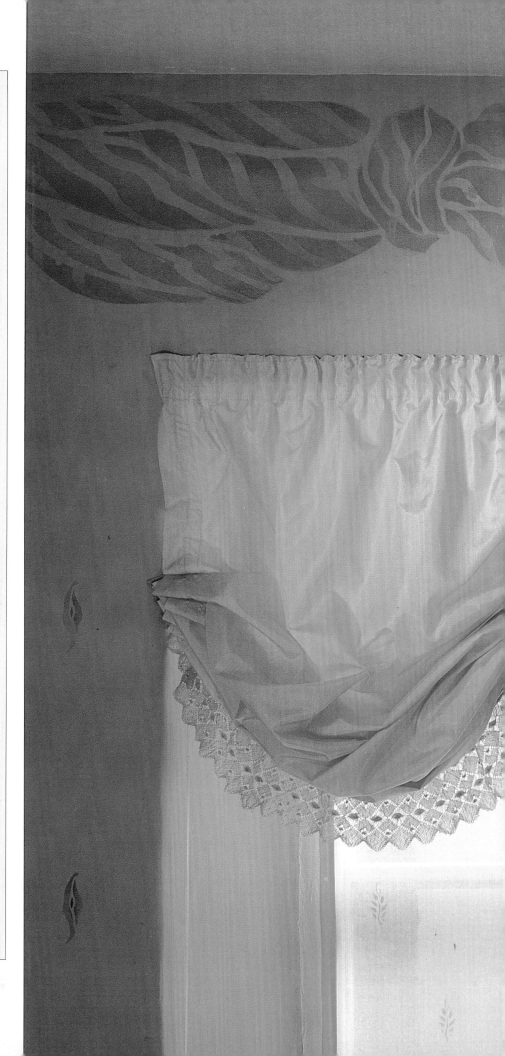

THE
SAMPLER BEDROOM

THIS NOT *very large bedroom is one of the attic rooms at the top of the house. It is a room that overhangs the narrow thoroughfare outside. Opposite the window there is a small narrow alleyway, which has beautiful cobbled pavings going along, with little tracks where cartwheels must have run inside the more higgledy-piggledy patterns of the cobbles, and this, coupled with the house across the street being so close, imparts a very intimate feeling to the bedroom.*

THE ROOM'S PHYSICAL FEATURES

The room's only window is set very low. It is a mere eight to ten inches off the floor and is flanked on each side by two narrow portions of wall. The balance is very delightful, with various cascading wooden planes of beams which eventually end as they slope up to the ceiling.

The ceiling itself is quite tiny compared to the scale of the room because three of the walls slant right into it at the top. Not one wall in this room is identical in height or size.

The main excitement of the room is that although being so intimate and low in feeling, it is large and spacious enough to easily house a four-poster bed. This sits happily on the one straight wall that there is; the one that reaches right up to the height of the ceiling, while the other walls sort of snuggle down around it.

On the opposite side to the straight wall, there is a very delightful little cast iron Victorian bedroom fireplace, and around it the most immensely crooked mantlepiece of delightful shape and simplicity. However, the main thing that you notice when you look at it is that it is extremely crooked, but this must be the charm of houses of this nature, that not one wall or any particular structure is square on.

Another intriguing part of this room is a little secret door cut into one of the walls. When you open it up, you spy an interior attic space formed over the barrel-shaped ceiling of the dining room below.

The entrance to the room is a very pretty little paneled door made up of two square panels, one above the other, hung with very beautiful old iron hinges. It sits quite simply, cut deeply indented, into one corner of the room, beside the bed, cutting in low on the corner.

With such a very extraordinary room there is a necessity to impose some formal structure over it, and that is why I decided to panel it.

The carnation border is on both the walls and the cloth of the quilt and canopy, while the honeysuckle border is used to decorate the panels of the fireplace.

THE DESIGN CONCEPT

I felt that samplers would be an interesting way to proceed, and it was from the simple imagery of cross-stitched samplers that I took my lead. I have an old sampler that belonged to my grandmother (I believe it was, in fact, stitched by an aunt of hers), that has a very pretty design around it of carnations or pinks. This is a very particular form of design that can be recognized as a sampler border, and I decided to use this to panel the room quite minutely.

The main project in this room is the stenciled quilt on the bed, and here I took my inspiration from an extremely amusing set of cross-stitched panels that I felt at the time to have been worked on a long time ago in Denmark. My delight in translating these into stencils was very much increased by the enjoyment of their wittiness at telling the story of love sought, won and enjoyed. Later on, I was absolutely astonished to discover from a Danish visitor who came to see me, that the cross-stitch panels had been stitched very recently by the Queen of Denmark. I was a little perturbed because whereas one is usually able to work directly on older designs where there is no question of copyright, in this case, I might be thought a little impertinent to interpret something so new. Luckily, however, I asked for, and received permission from the seamstress herself to translate her designs into stencils.

I also used all sorts of incidental cross-stitched designs that I had picked up from various other samplers, as well as some I made up to reflect my Cornish surroundings. This imagery is dotted around the bed – not just on the skirt of the cover, but also on the canopy and drapes.

Here the effects of intermingling the colors can be seen against the old plasterwork as the carnation border marks out "panels" on the bedroom walls.

112

COLOR MATCHING ON SURFACES

The material on which you stencil will affect the result. On a hard surface like a wall, every speck of color shows very clearly. The softer finish of fabric, however, acts as a blotter soaking up the paint so the result is not as sharp. Therefore, you have to use more paint, to get more color.

It is also necessary when using different colors, especially quite delicate shades, to prevent them mixing and producing a muddy appearance. A guard, cut from a spare piece of stencil card is effective in screening colors from each other. Without such help, the red and green flowers would have been a dull khaki.

1 A folded piece of card makes a good mask to shield the red used for the flowers from spreading onto the surrounding leaves.

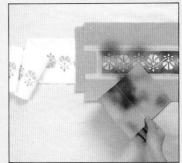

2 While here, the already sprayed part of the flowerhead is being covered, keeping it free from the green used, which might have a dulling effect on the image.

THE BED – ITS CANOPY
AND COVER

The fabric of the canopy, drapes and quilt is of a similar cream color as the walls, with a rustling texture similar to parchment.

The quilt is made of twelve panels, each one representing a month and the changing nature of the relationship depicted. Each panel was cut as a separate stencil, as was the trellised arch. By making the panels separately you avoid having to redo the quilt should you make a mistake on one. The stencils were then painted on to single pieces of cloth and these were subsequently stitched together with the carnation border running around the outside, and another rather more

tulip-like device running between the painted panels.

The skirt of the quilt was painted with individual stencil motifs based on a Cornish theme. There are baskets of pears, a vase of carnations, a boy holding a falcon aloft, a spotted dog, another vase of something that looks slightly like snapdragons, some fruit trees in a little pot, a unicorn and a lobster. These images were also used on the canopy at the top of the bed, which is cut and padded. They also appear on the cloth on the top of the bed and on the curtain at the back of the bed. The other curtains are left plain except for the carnation border and the curved tiebacks that are also padded and have the unicorn and a tulip design on them.

ABOVE The padded canopy presents an ideal area for stencilwork. The multi-colored piping is sprayed with stripes of the colors used for the imagery.

RIGHT The four-poster bed displaying all its incidental sampler imagery, ranging from the predictable pots of flowers to the more bizarre, lobsters and unicorns, and spotted dogs.

THE QUILT'S STORY

Told in twelve panels, the quilt depicts a suitor chasing a delightful girl that he sees while out skating in January. It carries through into their being at a masked ball in February. They then go on to meet by chance in a park in March; they meet once again out in the April showers, and by May he is on his knees under a bay tree, proposing to her. In June we see them getting wed, and in July we see them happily playing music in a garden under the trees. In August we see them both in harvest gear playing the peasants in a rather Marie Antoinette manner, and in September we have them happily picking pears from an espalier pear tree. October sees them out in their very smart shooting gear with their little gun dog, and in November they are enjoying the indoor life with mulled wine as he smokes his clay pipe. By December we have them hanging their Christmas decorations and gathering their parcels. And so we have the whole story of this young couple's life running through from their meeting right on to their finally settling into domesticity.

The quilt is made up of a number of handkerchief sized panels stenciled with the activities of a couple as they proceed through the months of the year. They are taken from contemporary needlework executed by the Queen of Denmark. The original crosswork designs are translated into stencils, then transferred onto separate pieces of cloth.

MAKING THE QUILT

The quilt consists of 12 panels. A tulip border was added to run between the panels and the sampler border runs along the edges. One whole strip with stenciled images was added to form the pillow end.

Once the top layer was assembled, I cut sufficient synthetic batting, and from the same fabric used for the top, a backing piece of the overall dimensions. I used French knots at the corner of each month to attach the three layers.

The skirt was made of three pieces. Each one was stenciled, backed and quilted separately then attached to the edging.

To make the stenciling quicker, I cut the framing piece separately and attached it to the individual images before spraying.

The skirt was meant to be cut in a curve, but it was much easier, and had the same effect, simply to stencil it as such on rectangular pieces.

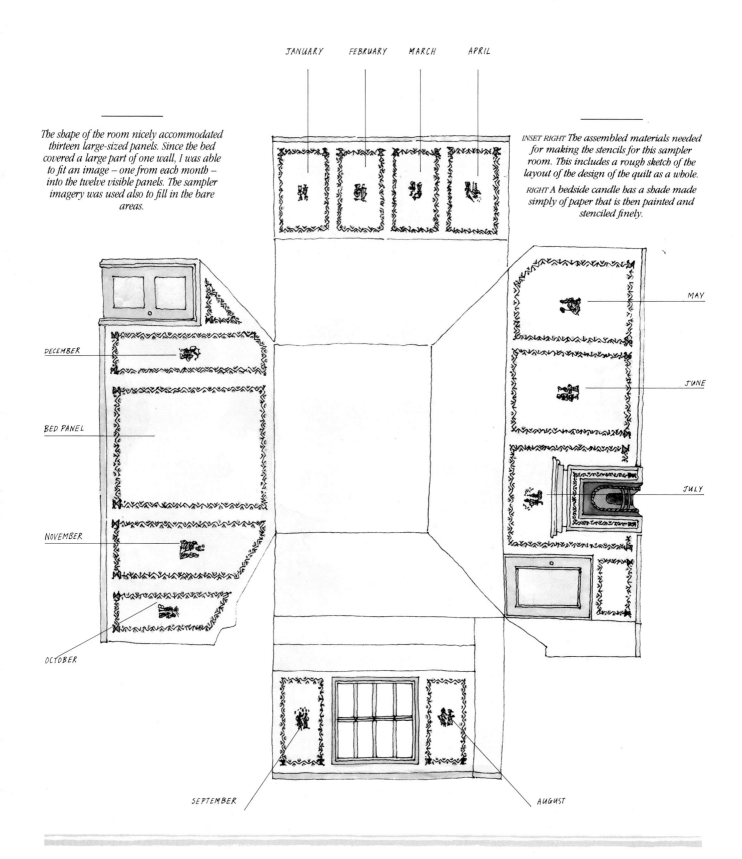

JANUARY   FEBRUARY   MARCH   APRIL

The shape of the room nicely accommodated thirteen large-sized panels. Since the bed covered a large part of one wall, I was able to fit an image – one from each month – into the twelve visible panels. The sampler imagery was used also to fill in the bare areas.

INSET RIGHT The assembled materials needed for making the stencils for this sampler room. This includes a rough sketch of the layout of the design of the quilt as a whole.

RIGHT A bedside candle has a shade made simply of paper that is then painted and stenciled finely.

DECEMBER

BED PANEL

NOVEMBER

OCTOBER

MAY

JUNE

JULY

SEPTEMBER

AUGUST

January – our lovers meet while out skating

February – in disguise, but still they recognize each other at a masked ball

March – out for a walk, is it just by chance that they meet?

April – the showery weather doesn't keep them apart

May – he's on his knees proposing and she appears to have accepted

June – at last they tie the knot and walk down the aisle

*July – at play in their own Garden of Eden,
perhaps*

*August – nature's bounty inspires a change
of costume*

*September – together they reap the harvest of
an abundant pear tree*

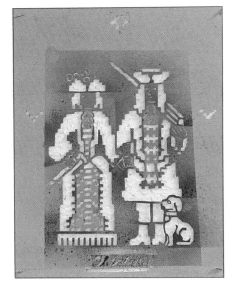

*October – more sporty pursuits outdoors
with the hunt in view*

*November – time for a chat together by the
fire with a warming drink and his pipe*

*December – preparing for Christmas –
hanging decorations and bearing presents*

The trellised arbor that frames the pair as they progress through the year, is a repeating motif that gives the quilt its formal structure, as well as providing an apt and appealing setting.

August

TOP RIGHT The wooden framed fabric of the fireplace incorporates a panel ideal for stenciling with a straggling honeysuckle design growing from a blue vase.

BELOW The month of July is depicted on the panel above rustic china on the mantlepiece.

RIGHT The month of August finds our pair depicted as harvesters, playing the peasant.

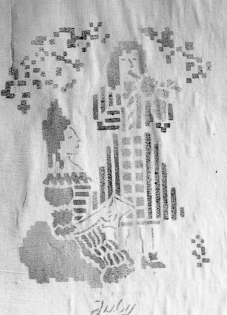

July

THE DECORATIVE TREATMENT

The final effect of the room was meant to be gentle. We used a pale cream paint on the walls, very soft and natural, that might be old whitewash. The walls are slightly warmer than if they had the usual whitewash which is often very white. Using the flower border stencil I paneled the walls – along most walls there are four panels, and these go to whatever height that particular wall reaches. At the bottom corner of each of these panels I placed a little vase from which the pink plant, which is very prolific indeed, grows. I used a similar device around the filleted panels of the fireplace, where there are two little vases each side. Out of these vases grow a similar border, but this time it is of honeysuckle. At the center top of the fireplace it meets in a slightly formal fleur-de-lys design. The leaves intertwine. The coloring on this is quite warm – the sort of colors that you associate with honeysuckle – creams touched with crimson.

When I had paneled out the walls of the room, I made sure that I had twelve visible panels because I thought it would be fun to put each of the little incidental meetings of our couple into the center of each panel of the wall. This I have done, and I feel that it is working well and gives the whole room

---

ABOVE Each curtain tie was cut out and stenciled before being made up.

RIGHT A panel before I added the motif of the month.

a quite delicate but definite sampler-like feeling. I very much like the juxta-position of stencilwork and needle-work, because I think they have so much in common in their designs.

The bedcover and the canopy and drapes were stenciled with the same images. It isn't always possible to use the same stencil on fabric as for grander surfaces such as walls. How-ever, in this case, the bed could be treated as a large-scale object so we did not have to alter the size of the stencil. Large amounts of fabric nor-mally require stronger patterns.

I painted the floor pale gray and the furniture of the room generally is of quite a dark rich mahogany color. There is a chest in the room that is stenciled with a more robust form of needlework in mind, that of crewel-work, and it has an all-over design of a tree of life just reaching over its curved top and in the center of the front panel, underneath the lock, is a big tree with a serpent in it, and underneath it Adam and Eve. The chest was painted a warm golden chrome yellow, and it looks well with the similar colors in the room. Otherwise we have some little bits of china around – just the sort that you would expect to find in an old attic bedroom in a house of any age.

Altogether the room has the gentle, warm, creamy look – fresh and yet not too cold – for our misty, sometimes quite gray Cornish days.

ABOVE Where the eaves of the house swoop down low to the wall, the top of the stenciled 'panels' have to accommodate and reflect this angle.

THE
DAY NURSERY

T HE DAY *nursery is up in the attic next door to the night nursery. It is one of a group of three rooms which have canopied ceilings. I imagined the day nursery as a treasure house for children – chock full of toys and games for them to fill the daylight hours. There's plenty of scope for invention and adventure...*

THE DECORATIVE
TREATMENT

The coloring in here is fairly bright; I mean in that I have used blues, golds, greens, terracottas, sugary pink, dark green, and fairly bright yellow. However, although I am using a full spectrum of color, the hues are also subdued. Because there is so much imagery here, I didn't want it to be overbearing. I just wanted it to be like a reminder of children's illustration – an exciting sort of imagery for small people to wander round, as though they were living in a picture book.

At one side of the room there is a green cupboard with doors with drawers underneath. It is a soft gray-green and on the doors of this cupboard I have stenciled a small garden fork and trowel with some leaves. This isn't a particularly childlike image, but it does seem to fit terribly well with the small trees. You can imagine that these little tools might be used for the sort of garden in which these trees might be found. On the lower part of this cupboard, the drawers have just a

few little leaves stenciled on them. At the sides we have more leaves – just a handful, so that it all adds to the imagery of being in a small garden.

On the fireguard we have painted across its actual wires to lighten it and to make it a pretty trellis shape in the room. This again adds to the garden feel of the imagery.

I liberally scattered the room with toys and books. In it I placed a table with a big checkered cloth surrounded by little chairs on which children can sit and do their own stenciling with watercolor, or look at books or play with plasticene.

On the floor there is an old round wooden hat-box which has been stenciled with rather circus-like motifs of stars (that echo the ceiling) and jagged lines to resemble the edge of a circus ring. This makes a very jolly sort of container for the toys that are scattered on the floor.

Beside the fireplace we have a nursery tea set up with bears and Babar the elephant, and there is a small tray set with boiled eggs and toast soldiers, one imagines.

Picture-book imagery adorns each complex surface of the old walls in this endearing room. The canopied roof becomes a sky and the lower portion of the walls a small garden, edged with shells.

THE DESIGN CONCEPT

The theme of this day nursery is, not unexpectedly, nursery rhymes. Above the baseboards of the room we have the cockleshells and around the dado level we have silver bells tied in bunches with blue ribbons. The bells link across, at quite a high dado level, so that they work well with the fireplace. Between the dado level and the baseboard we can get in the tree with "a silver nutmeg and a golden pear" of the nursery rhyme. These sit in pretty terracotta pots and would actually be the height of most average toddlers.

Above the dado, regularly spaced around the room, we have images of a quite fragile ring of roses. Up above them, as we reach up into the canopied ceiling, we have a mottled ceiling, the rich blue of an Arabian night, scattered with stars. The blue was daubed on in two stages: first a strong blue, then a paler tone for depth.

On one side of the ceiling there is a curved thin new moon with a face in it – the Man in the Moon looking down. One of the stars on one of the side panels is particularly large, and that is the twinkling star in "Twinkle, twinkle, little star". I suppose it shouldn't be large, it should be smaller.

On a higher level of the wall, spaced out across its undulating surface are the rings of roses from the nursery rhyme.

THE ROOM'S PHYSICAL
FEATURES

Each of the walls is unbelievably undulating, and the actual texture of the
walls from the old plaster is very tactile
indeed. It's a surface that is an absolute
joy to stencil because the stencil ad-
heres to that undulating surface very
well, and yet you have that particular
feel of an old wall that has been left as
is rather than straightened and remade
into some sort of standard quality for it
to take a wallpaper or other finish. It is
the loveliest wall I have worked on
apart from the Carolean wall at Nether
Lypiatt in Gloucester. I am extremely
interested in working on such surfaces
because I think it makes the stenciling

far more tactile than on new plaster.

At the top of each of these walls is a
little ledge that runs in from the wall
into the center of the room, and this is
supported by some very good sturdy,
uneven, angular beams. This little lip
to the top of each wall then extends up
and into the really very unusual canopied ceiling that gives the room its
character and charm. The ceiling
reaches to a height of some four to five
feet further up, and in the center of the
room as you look up, there is this little
oblong which is, in fact, the flat part of
the ceiling left once the other walls
have sloped in to it. An interesting
aside is that the medieval word for
stenciling is "estellis" – "to star", and
therefore it is particularly apt that I

*LEFT The Man in the Moon in a bright night
sky is surrounded by yellow stars.*

*ABOVE The same star stencil looks more
circus-like under the lid of a round wooden
toy box, which also had a zig zag edge
stenciled around the top.*

THE STENCIL SCHEME

This room plan of the Day Nursery shows how densely the imagery is packed in this small light room. Plenty for the young imagination to feed on.

FAR RIGHT This is the complete set of stencils cut for decorating the nursery. They show that even a quite densely stenciled room needs comparatively few actual stencils to achieve its effects.

RIGHT A small side window looks down the street towards the church tower and the sea. On the sill is a Swiss chalet made out of cigar box wood as a souvenir for travelers to Europe.

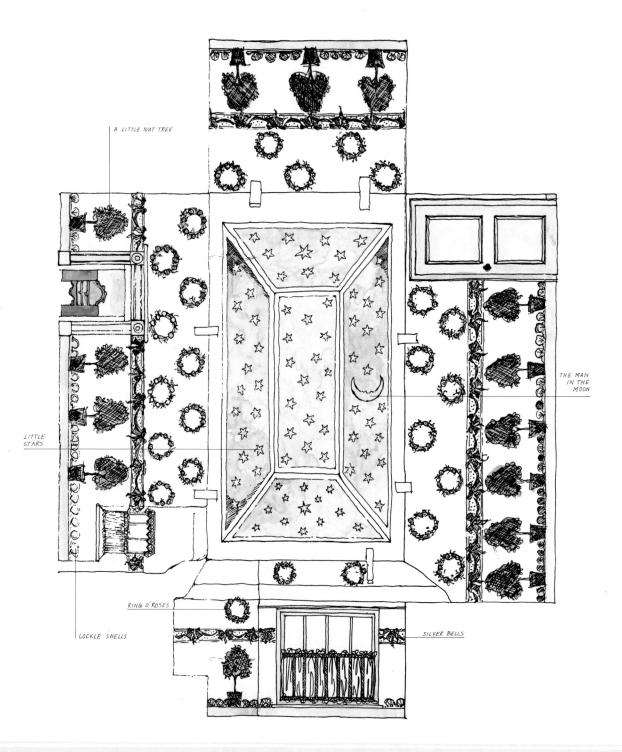

A LITTLE NUT TREE

THE MAN IN THE MOON

LITTLE STARS

RING O' ROSES

COCKLE SHELLS

SILVER BELLS

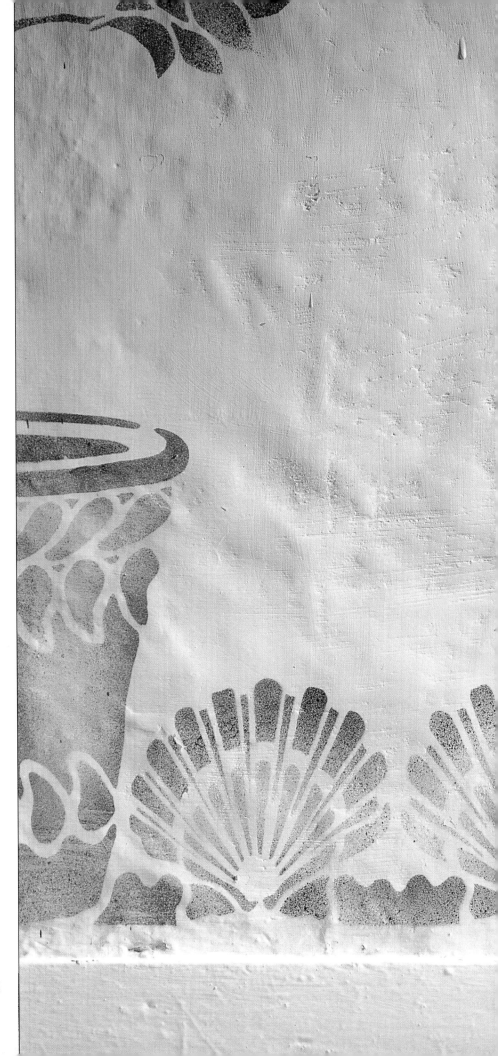

should be stenciling stars on this ceiling just as the medieval halls were covered with stars.

The room also contains a very pretty fireplace. It is quite formal and Victorian. It has a high basket-shaped grate covered with little cast iron flowers and leaves – an absolute joy – and ideal for sitting round and having a delicious tea.

The door is at the far end of the room, and there are two windows. One window has the usual sort of rhythm that we find in these rooms – situated eight inches off the floor with low cascading angular beams coming down to meet it at the top. The window has nursery bars to stop any children hanging out of it, as it hangs over this steep little street. The room has this lovely low light coming into it, flooding over the floor. Quite close to this window is another incredible little window, set into a corner in the side of the house. It is quite tiny, but it looks down towards the sea and there is a most exquisite view. Through it I can see the morning sun coming up over the tower of the church, and the other roofs, sideways on as you look down Chapel Street. The window is set quite deeply into the wall which is itself some eighteen inches thick, and it has a very extraordinary complicated head to it, as the cut in of the window tries to meet the complexity of the ceiling. We get the most bizarre shapes there, totally unarchitectural in any form or sense of the word. Such shapes are ideal for stenciled decoration as you can fit stencils into strange shapes. I

Above the baseboard, interspersed by pots of fruit trees, are set out even rows of cockleshells while at a higher level are strung up rows of silver bells. They both come from the nursery rhyme

"Mary Mary quite contrary
How does your garden grow?
With silver bells and cockleshells
And Pretty Maids all in a row."

136

have, in fact, fitted a stencil into a shape there where it does do what stenciling can do – make rather a pig's ear bit of architecture into something that actually seems quite right and absolutely correct.

There are baseboards along all the walls of the room and, in fact, on one wall, this baseboard rises four inches and drops right down into the corner. Four inches is a very large amount for a small wall to change. I had to consider how I would be able to balance this out visually by getting the lines working. This became a juggle when placing the borders, one along the top of the baseboard and the other along the dado, and just easing the difference in from one corner by lifting one border two inches rather than the four inches so the discrepancy is less emphasized.

Teddy Bears picnic in front of a warming fire.

STENCILING UP TO A FIREPLACE

It's important, in order to avoid a blurred image, not to stencil directly into the recess when you bring stenciled imagery to a fireplace. It is impossible to get the stencil to sit flat when you tuck it under the mantle shelf; you must leave a gap. Since the stencil is brought to the fireplace only when the rest of the painting has been done, its very important that you accurately place the rest of the dado.

1 In order to give the trees a fair height, the bells were lined up with the top part of the fireplace. They had to fit snugly up to and under the mantle shelf.

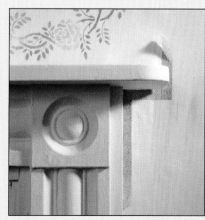

2 Masking tape was fixed flat against the wall right up to the edge of the mantlepiece to provide the necessary gap.

3 The stencil was then placed over it and sprayed. This ensured that the design finished cleanly and abruptly, without blurring and fading away.

THE TOY CUPBOARD

On each of the clearly defined panels there is a trowel and fork backed by bunches of bay leaves tied up with garden twine; these contribute to the feeling of the miniature garden here.

The background color was produced by rubbing grayish-white paint over a slightly sharper green than the finished result.

On each of the two drawers there is a sprig of box tree leaf and this again is tied with golden garden twine. The leaves also decorate each of the rather ample corners of the panels of the door. Quite often this isn't a big enough area to decorate, but since the panels are curved there is a good space for some decoration. On each of the long sides of the cupboard there is a group of tied leaves, slightly larger than any of the other groupings, while a shallower group is repeated on its flat top. With this treatment, the whole of the cupboard does appear to have this gentle leaf imprint in a darker bluish green stamped across its paler surface presenting a rustic look. There is some soft gray paint very casually strewn over the inside of the cupboard that might well be termed bad paint-work but, in fact, looks as if someone just did it a long time ago.

The miniature trowel and fork that make up the design for these cupboard doors are not necessarily toy-like, but they seem to feel at home in this room. The cupboard is painted the color of sage and has small bunches of this herb stenciled on each side panel.

141

THE
NIGHT NURSERY

WAY UP *above the noise of the street, in one of the small but high rooms, we placed the night nursery. It is an intimate room with a peaceful vaulted ceiling. Calmness and security are what the room should hold. Just as a mother bird folds her wing protectively over her sleeping chicks, the high ceiling seems to represent an encompassing embrace, a bower in which small innocents dream away safe from harm.*

THE DESIGN CONCEPT

The stencil decoration was designed to accentuate the room's ceiling, its most unusual feature, playing it up to the full with tiers of leafy borders. On each of the ceiling's four sloping sides is a centrally-placed cameo shape containing a dove of peace. The sprig of leaves in the dove's beak carries through the theme of the bolder-scaled leafy border.

The decoration was to be concentrated on the ceiling not just because of its particularly appealing structure, but also because it would provide interest for wakeful children as they lay in their beds gazing upwards. The imagery was chosen with a view to providing reassurance.

The color scheme was also to be undemanding – soft gray-green leaves, muted pink ribbons, misty blue birds and old ocher lettering.

In choosing the dove as an image for this room used for sleeping, I was aware of its soothing connotations of peace, hope and promise – the dove returning to the Ark with the olive branch that told of land and safety.

This was also the intention of the name stencils that I wanted to place above each bed. This naming of a sleeping place is, in essence, a Scandinavian idea for the decoration of a child's room. Traditionally carried out in freehand paintwork, it lends itself well to stenciling.

The emphasis of the decoration in this room would be concentrated at eye level and above, so adding a stenciled canvas floor covering seemed appropriate. Not only would it bring some of the imagery into play at ground level, it would soften also the austerity of the pale, bare boards.

The nursery is a suitable place for a floor covering because here it does not have to withstand heavy use. Such a setting provides an appropriate opportunity to display, what is after all, one of the most delightful of stenciled artifacts.

As I worked on the design, it all began to piece together gradually, and acquired an atmosphere of gentleness and simplicity suited to the room and its use.

A medallion of leaves encircling a dove decorates the sides of the vaulted ceiling in the nursery. A stencil hangs above the crib proclaiming the name of its night-time occupant, Jack.

143

THE DECORATIVE
TREATMENT

It seemed appropriate to apply a rich creamy latex to the beautifully undulating old plasterwork of the walls, in imitation of basic whitewash. This provides a simple foil for the room, counterbalancing the intrinsically ornate quality of the stencilwork.

In order to create the leafy canopy on the ceiling, larger branches were drawn and connected together, curving up at intervals as they linked up around the base.

The decorative bordering is built up by using one basic stencil element, a straight, slender branch. The leaves that start away from its middle notch have a natural look, and are not always the same number on each side. On the lowest border, the pink ribbon is used to form a linking device, which allows for adjustments to be made while positioning it evenly around the room. Above this it is simply a question of one leaf tip meeting another to effect this rhythm. This also simplifies the process of the design turning at a corner, for as long as the branches end up somewhere near this junction they will form a visual link across it. Usually the problem of turning a design at a corner involves more complicated adjustments, sometimes a special stencil has to be made to achieve this. With this scheme small amounts of pink ribbon are sometimes introduced among the leaves above particular stencil devices "tying" them in.

The personalized motifs are attached to the leaf frieze by a long pink ribbon. A heart is also incorporated into the design as a whole, tied to the ribbon.

LEFT The dove with its olive branch is one of four that decorate each wall of the steeply sloping ceiling.

RIGHT The unusual inverted ledge effect at the top of each wall of this old room provides an opportunity for a double layer of leaf borders.

THE STENCIL SCHEME

Basically the scheme for this room is formed from five separate stencil elements, three of which are simple and repeated often; the other two are more complicated and used sparingly. They are the simple curved ribbon link (used in conjunction with the shorter of the two branch lengths), the long and short branch lengths, the name stencil and the dove stencil. The latter has attached to it the specially curved branches which join it into the main border design.

While the bordering of the ceiling is kept to the simple leaf design, the frieze running around the main walls is injected with further form and color by interspersing links of pink ribbon.

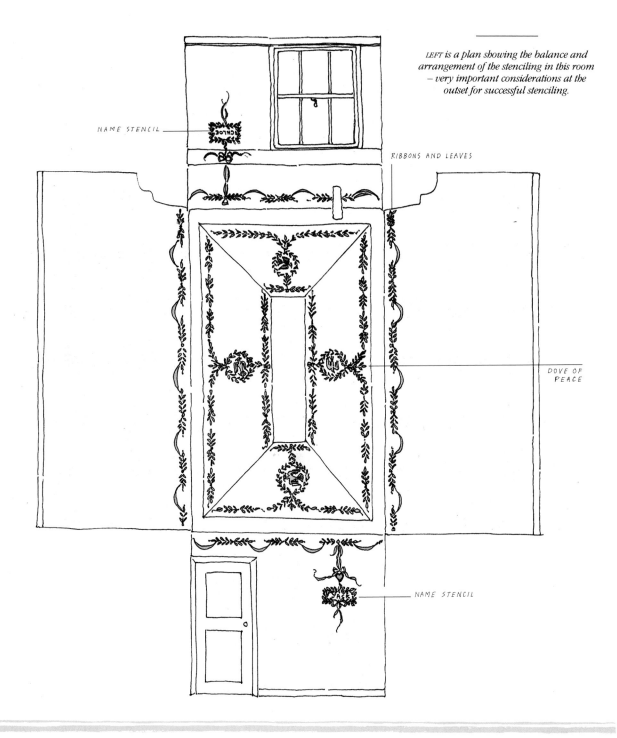

NAME STENCIL

RIBBONS AND LEAVES

LEFT is a plan showing the balance and arrangement of the stenciling in this room – very important considerations at the outset for successful stenciling.

DOVE OF PEACE

NAME STENCIL

The floor covering was stenciled with the same branches and ribbons as the walls. The piece of sailcloth was turned under and double hemmed before it was painted. I drew a plan of the images beforehand and followed this when I later sprayed them directly on the cloth. I then placed heavy brown paper under the cloth to protect the floor before applying the varnish which would otherwise seep through. I used one coat of clear polyurethane matte varnish, making certain I had sufficient fresh varnish to complete the cloth. The floor covering was then left to dry before I removed the paper.

The border pattern is sprayed onto another sheet of stencil card to form a frame. The letters of the name are carefully spaced out into the blank slot. They are mapped out in pencil for ease of adjustment. The middle letter or letters of the name are placed in the center first, in order to achieve an approximate even spacing of the letter either side. Using a dark felt-tip pen the letter is washed across so that the different strokes are separated into shapes that can be cut away while the basic letter forms are retained.

1 To personalize the name stencil, begin by spraying the framing for the name stencil onto a wall, over a bed, if you wish.

2 Place the border portion of this stencil over a similar sized sheet of stencil card.

3 Spray the design through onto the lower sheet in order to create a frame.

4 Draw in the child's name and cut it out. Also cut out two leaves as position guides.

5 Place the stencil on the wall, lining it up with the leaves painted on the wall.

6 Spray over the cut-out letters of the name and stencil in a contrasting color.

The completed name stencil, an idea
adapted from a Swedish custom where a
child's name hangs above its sleeping
place. The ribbon could change from pink
to blue if it is more appropriate.

THE ROOM'S PHYSICAL FEATURES

The room itself, however, presented some challenges. Although this is one of the smallest rooms in the house it is still spacious, and with its extended canopied ceiling, tall. It is very simple in layout with a low window at one end of the room and a small door at the other.

The room's claim to charm is due entirely to its rustic vaulted ceiling – most unexpected in such a basically unpretentious setting.

Low light comes in at the window and emphasizes the texture of the beautiful old plasterwork, creamy and undulating. Altogether the room makes an enticing subject for setting to on the craft of stenciling.

It was important that the stenciled name should hang at the head of the bed, as it did quite easily over the crib on the opposing wall. While the bed fitted snugly in beside the window, it was situated under an additional jutting beam. This presented a problem. I solved it by slicing the stencil in three and applying it flatly to each perpendicular surface so that while there is a break in the stencil, it does carry on at a slightly lower level. Trouble was taken to line up the design straight – one piece exactly above the other. This avoided any uncomfortable jumbling of the hanging images of ribbons, leaves, hearts and name tag.

Further along the same wall a supporting beam breaks into the flow of the frieze. I stenciled this to look as if the border continues under the area of the beam in order not to break up the rhythm of the design.

Adaptability is one of the great benefits of stenciling. No surface is too complicated to encompass with its wily patterns. It can curve down and around beams and leap from one surface to another.

THE TECHNIQUES OF
STENCILING

A small stool was enlivened by the addition of a bright central sun. Wood, as long as it is in good condition, is an ideal surface.

A fanciful palm tree graces the wooden surface of the linen cupboard in the bathroom. The enamel-based paint withstands moisture well.

A fairly imperial wreath was stenciled on the cast iron surface of the old bath. Commercially-available reconditioning paint was used first.

The flowing rhythm of the ribbons encircle a very pretty posy that decorates what was previously an undistinguished table.

In decorating the blanket chest I drew on the connection of traveling trunks and these docile beasts of burden about to amble off.

Wooden pelmets were designed to make rather plain windows much more individual. I matched them with different-sized stencils.

Even a rather ordinary piece of reproduction furniture can be transformed into something quite elaborate. I stenciled the inside as well.

Stenciling looks especially good on surfaces that have a texture. The uneven plaster walls in this house were a perfect background.

Fabric is easy to stencil and, in the case of cushions such as these, you can produce something quite effective without much effort.

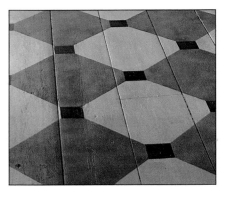

Stencils can be put to more than one use. The stars in this toybox were also used to decorate the ceiling in the same room.

Small details, such as this section of the dining room mantlepiece, benefit from stenciling just as much as larger areas.

Using my method, a stenciled floor can add a great deal to the impression a room makes; small spaces appear much grander.

Stenciled shades are easy to do especially if you use ready-made ones. Here, I've coordinated the window with the wall treatment.

More extensive lengths of fabric, such as these floor-length bed drapes look very effective stenciled. They can be dry-cleaned.

Stencil card can also be used to make lamp and candleshades. If painted, the translucent surface looks very charming with light behind it.

The solid color fabric strips on these cushions have been spray painted as has the cane mesh of the chairs and sofa.

Stenciled floorcloths make attractive coverings for floors. Once painted they should be varnished to protect against heavy wear.

The velvet covering of the fireboard produced a final effect that is much more attractive than what it looked like when I used plasterboard.

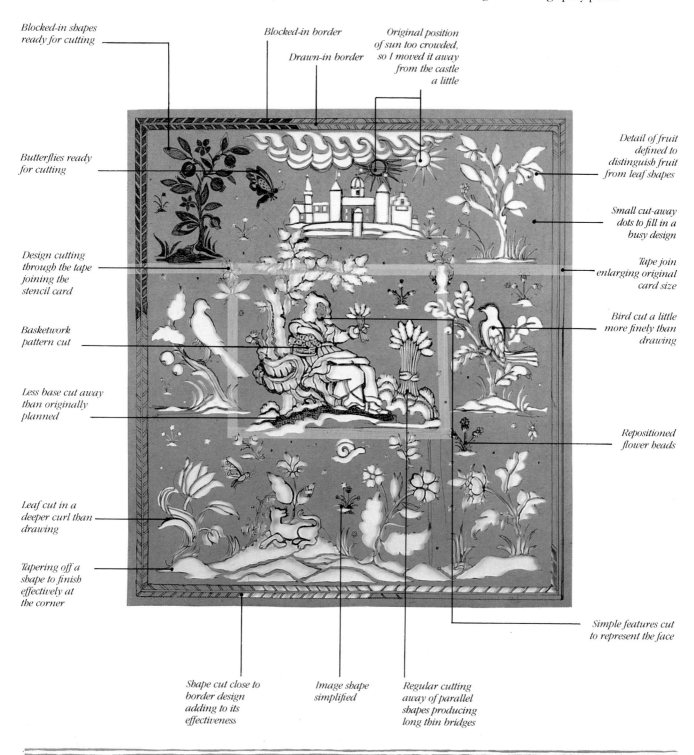

WORK IN PROGRESS

On the following pages I have set out everything you need to know to stencil successfully whether you use commercially available stencils or design your own. Below is a good example of what most stencils look like while they are being worked on. Many of my images have changed shape or position, and over-enthusiastic cutting has resulted in a patch or two. To see the final result, refer to the Sitting Room fireboard on page 78. On the next three pages I demonstrate, as best I can in a static medium, my technique of applying color using spray paint.

Blocked-in shapes ready for cutting

Blocked-in border

Drawn-in border

Original position of sun too crowded, so I moved it away from the castle a little

Detail of fruit defined to distinguish fruit from leaf shapes

Butterflies ready for cutting

Small cut-away dots to fill in a busy design

Design cutting through the tape joining the stencil card

Tape join enlarging original card size

Basketwork pattern cut

Bird cut a little more finely than drawing

Less base cut away than originally planned

Repositioned flower heads

Leaf cut in a deeper curl than drawing

Tapering off a shape to finish effectively at the corner

Simple features cut to represent the face

Shape cut close to border design adding to its effectiveness

Image shape simplified

Regular cutting away of parallel shapes producing long thin bridges

156

FINISHED
STENCILWORK

*Simply with three colors, basic green, blue
and yellow, a lively image has emerged. The
mingling particles of paint sprayed across
the surface of the stencils selectively produced
this mellow effect. Afterwards, to integrate the
stencilwork more with the surface, I lightly
daubed over it with some white latex
paint. The simple stages that produced
this attractive result are shown overleaf.*

————

TOP LEFT With the stencil in position, and carefully screened around with guards, it is ready for coloring.

BOTTOM LEFT AND CENTER A dark green is selected for the basic vine leaf color and selectively sprayed onto various areas. A hand-held guard is positioned briefly to protect the grapes from the very dark color. Some leaves are sprayed more intensely than others to introduce life-like variations.

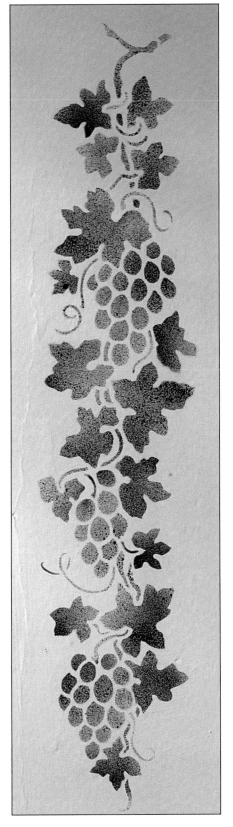

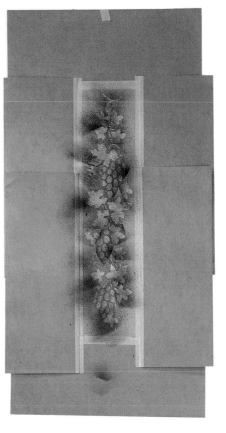

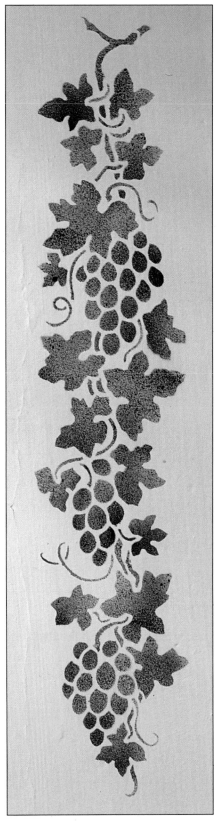

OPPOSITE AND LEFT The next color is a deep blue. This is allowed to spray over the bunches of grapes, lightly tinting them. It also coats some of the leaves making the already darker ones even denser in tone. The stems and tendril shapes of the design are also picking up the blue at this stage.

TOP AND RIGHT The third color used to complete this stenciled vine is gold yellow ocher. This does its usual job of enlivening the image, tinting the leaves an autumnal hue, ripening up a few grapes and turning the stems into the color of wood.

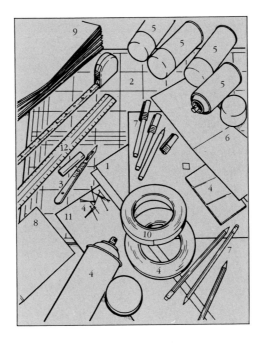

MATERIALS

1 STENCIL CARD: Manila, soaked in lin-seed oil, makes the best stencils. It is pliable and easy to cut but also substantial and tough.

2 CUTTING BOARD: Made of special material to withstand cut lines, it provides an even and protective finish even after prolonged use. The color is useful for making your image stand out and to show up any weak areas.

3 CRAFT KNIFE: A sharp blade and sturdy handle is necessary for even cutting. A protective cap should be fitted when it is not in use. In-expensive disposable ones are readily available.

4 FIXING MATERIALS: Aerosol adhesive, pins or adhesive putty can all be used to apply the stencil to a sur-face firmly but temporarily.

5 SPRAY PAINT: Push-button aerosol paint is versatile and easy to apply. I use Plasti-Kote paints that are free of fluorocarbons.

6 PAPER MASK: This should be used when working with aerosols in confined areas.

7 PENCILS AND PENS: Eraser-topped pencils and felt-tip pens are needed to produce drawings on paper and card.

8 GUARDS: Small remnants of card are used to direct paint accurately.

9 NEWSPAPER OR LINING PAPER: This should be used to mask off areas from paint.

10 MASKING TAPE: An invaluable aid used to fix stencils firmly, repair mistakes, attach masking paper and join pieces of stencil card together.

11 SKETCH PAD: This is used to draw up your initial design. Both large and small pads are useful.

12 MEASURING DEVICES: A tape measure and ruler may both be needed to draw up designs as well as to posi-tion them properly.

Stenciling supplies by mail order from:
LYN LE GRICE STENCIL DESIGN LTD
Bread Street, Penzance, TR18 2EQ
England

Stencils
Stencil designs
Oiled Manilla card
Craft knives
Stencil prints
Stenciling books
Mail order catalogue (£1)

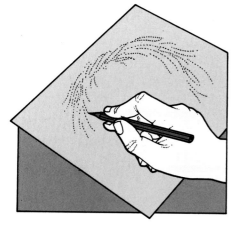

Begin your drawing on paper with pencil so that you can easily correct the shapes as you go.

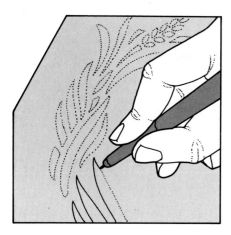

Flatten and simplify your shapes. Then change to a felt-tip pen to make clearer their outlines.

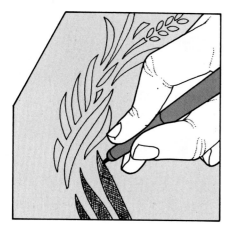

Work into the area to be cut out with cross-hatching. This will cause your shapes to stand out clearly.

DRAWING UP A DESIGN

You might like to begin by making several sketches – experimenting with the shapes involved until you arrive at a satisfactory composition. Even if you don't consider yourself very good at drawing, almost anyone can create a successful stencil. Begin with something simple – one large image – and then add a border to create further complexity.

As you work on your drawings, simplify the shapes by flattening and broadening areas so they can be cut out as a flat pattern. Use a pencil to begin with so you can correct your drawing easily. Once you've worked out a possible design, use a pen to outline those areas that you will be cutting away; cross-hatching will help these shapes to stand out.

CUTTING BRIDGES

While it is true that your image will be seen only through the areas that are cut away, the intact areas are an integral part of the appeal. A lot of the charm of stencilwork comes from the rhythmic frequency of these linking pieces or *bridges*. These are as vital to the design as the cut-away areas. Bridges must be seen as part of the design; for the best result, they should be cut in the spirit of the rest of the images – if the design contains curves, they can curve as well. For instance, you will need to break up long, flowing lines that can occur when your design includes grasses or ribbons. But you can maintain their effect by using a regular diagonal slant for the bridges.

Besides being part of the design, bridges are necessary to maintain the integrity of your stencil; they hold it together in one piece. It is essential that they occur at regular intervals, otherwise the stencil would fall apart.

The amount and thickness of the

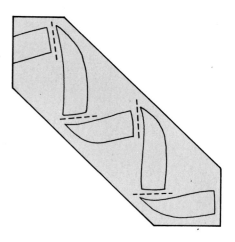

Maintain the flow of your design by spacing sufficient bridges of adequate size in a regular rhythm.

Wider, more substantial bridges are needed when large areas of card are cut away.

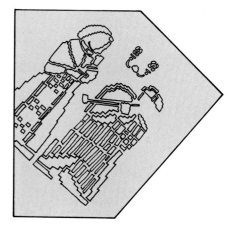

Finer, more frequent bridges are used in more detailed and complicated designs.

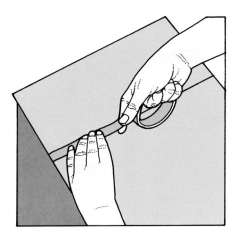

If you have to join pieces of card, butt them up close and secure with a strip of masking tape across each side.

Preserve a margin of space around the planned image by drawing a frame of sufficient size.

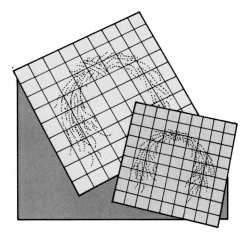

A grid system can be used to scale up a design. Transfer each element in a small square to a larger one.

bridges depends on your design. To maintain the flow of your image, they should be of a similar size. When large areas of card are to be cut away, wider bridges will be necessary, while a finely-detailed design can be maintained with more delicate bridges. However, if a bridge is too thin it may prove too delicate to hold the design together while in use.

DRAWING ON CARD

If your image is too large to fit on a single piece of card, you will have to join one or more pieces for the required size. Butt the pieces up close together, leaving no gap as you may well want to cut shapes through this area. Use masking tape on both sides of the join and press it down flat. Don't wrap tape around the join as it will make the cutting surface too thick.

You also have to leave a margin of space around the cut-out image, so draw your frame before you start.

Begin with a pencil and work on the design until you are satisfied, then change to a felt-tip pen, which is more visible and flows freely over the card's surface. Block in the shapes as you did on the paper drawing, making certain that in complicated areas it is quite clear where you will be cutting. If your drawing is to be done to a larger size, you can scale up the image by using a grid. Transfer each individual element falling within a smaller square on your drawing to a proportionally larger square on the card.

Many people find a photocopy machine useful in scaling a design up or down in order to transfer it.

CUTTING YOUR STENCIL

If you are not using a special cutting board, you still need to work on a strong, durable surface; a piece of hardboard would be ideal. You also need a good craft knife or a scalpel with a new blade.

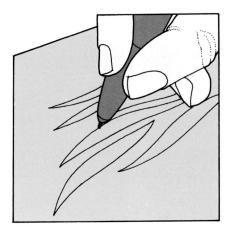

Felt-tip pens show up well on stencil card and should be used to outline your drawing.

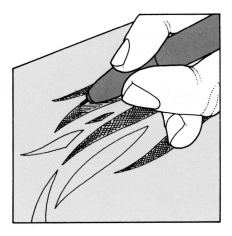

Block in the shapes you will be cutting out. They should be clearly visible, especially in complicated areas.

Start cutting from the middle outwards and cut out smaller shapes before the surrounding larger ones.

Make certain to cut along the outer edge of your blocked-in area to maintain the clarity of the design.

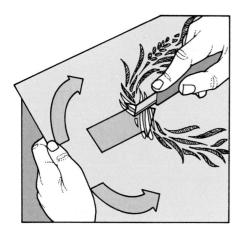

Always cut towards yourself. You will have to turn the stencil continually as you go.

If you make a mistake – like cutting into a bridge – repair it with a small piece of masking tape.

Always start cutting from the middle of your design so that you are not working across cut shapes. This is not only uncomfortable but cut-out areas are thus put at risk of being damaged. It is also a good idea to cut out smaller shapes before larger ones. Small shapes tend to get isolated and, if you cut them out after you've cut out much larger areas surrounding them, it is quite easy for the blade to slip and cause damage. Always cut along the outer edge of the blocked-in area so the design stands out clearly and the flow of the design is maintained.

Turn the stencil as you go so that you always cut towards yourself. This makes the process easier. If you find that your arm gets tired, relax your shoulder and elbow; you should work only from the wrist. Always apply a steady, even pressure as you proceed. In time, you will develop a fluidity that will enable you to cut shapes with a certain verve.

If you make a mistake, such as cutting off a bridge, you can patch the area with a small piece of masking tape sealed on both sides of the card. Make certain the tape does not cover any cut-out areas.

BORDERS

All border patterns should consist of repeating motifs. It is important, since the stencil will be positioned all around an area, that the stencil is accurately designed to produce a continuous, unbroken effect. In almost all cases, borders are repositioned again and again; therefore, the right-hand end of the stencil, when joined to the left-hand end, must match exactly.

An easy way to ensure this continuity is to draw a length of border design on your stencil card. Leave several inches blank at one end. Clarify your design and then cut out the first 3 to 4 inches.

Now bend the piece of card around to form a loop, sliding one end under

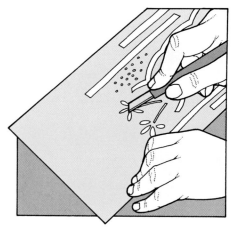

When designing stencil borders, draw up to the last few inches, leaving the end blank. Cut out the first 3–4 inches.

With the cut piece on top, slide the other end under forming a loop. Notice how the design flows.

Now draw through the cut-out pieces onto the blank end to form your matching linking shapes.

As you paint, position your stencil over the matching end of a finished length. Mask the cut-out end when you spray.

To make a corner piece for your border, draw two right angles the width of your stencil apart.

the other, with the cut piece on top, until you see how the design is flowing.

When you get to the end, draw through the cut pieces to make the linking shapes. Then cut these out to complete the border.

Later on, when you are painting the border, you use the repeated elements as a position guide. After starting in the corner and spraying the first length of border, reposition the border stencil, aligning the identical elements at the end. Cover this cut-out area with masking tape and/or a guard, and then spray the next length of border.

CORNER AND LINK PIECES

Should your border be used both horizontally and vertically, you will need to cut a corner piece. First measure the width of your stencil. Then, on a square piece of card draw a right angle. Draw another right angle the measured distance away so that you end up with an L-shape the width of your border stencil.

Leave the corner blank but place your cut stencil on each side and either draw or spray the pattern on to the card. Then draw in a corner motif to link the two ends effectively.

In those instances where you need to bridge two areas but your stencil does not fit exactly, you will have to cut another stencil. An easy way to do this is to use a blank length of card to cover the remaining space. With your stencil in place, spray the end of this length and repeat for the other side. Then adjust your design to fit in the available space. Any discrepancies should not be noticeable.

SURFACE PREPARATION

Most surfaces require only the minimum of preparation before you can apply your stencils. The important factors are that the surface be intact, and if colored, complementary.

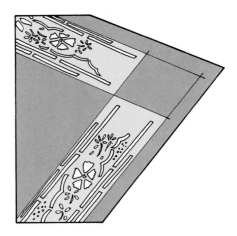

Then draw in or spray through your pattern on the other side of the corner.

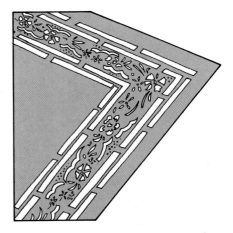

Finally, in the corner, draw in a version of your pattern that will link the two sides; then cut it out.

Daub a painted wall with a slightly lighter or darker tone, to provide an attractive background.

RIGHT These sails have been worked out by paying close attention to the authentic set of the sails on old sailing ships: how many for each mast and which ones overlapped which. Finely cut lines were used to create the network of rigging.

BELOW Intricate small pieces are cut regularly away to achieve this basketwork effect. It is well worth the time working out the structure of an actual basket weave in order to create this impression convincingly.

RIGHT In order to merge the fox with his background, leaves are cut that seem to overlay the large shape of his body. They also perform the function of providing a convenient intercepting device between two large cut-away areas.

LEFT The realistic folding ribbon design zig zagging around the edge of this table top was achieved by starting the bridges to define the folds. The less structured form of the bows also employs this method to achieve depth.

RIGHT This stencil was cut to provide a medallion for the bathroom ceiling and uses the blank yet functional center as the apex of the design. In order to position this stencil you need to feed it over the hanging light fixture.

RIGHT It is difficult to form a face from cut-out stencil pieces as there is a need both to cut away the whole outlined shape of a face and, in addition, individual features. A passable image, however, can be achieved with a few deftly chosen lines, of the most prominent features.

LEFT Judicious cutting was necessary to separate out the pear shapes from the leaves. Fairly robust bridges were used to hold this large-scale design.

ABOVE "Overlapping" shapes can add dimension to an image, and produce, overall, a more dense and compact shape.

LEFT The repeat of the rope in two different scales adds to the effectiveness of this design. While the complicated "bridgework" at each junction of the anchor adds to its authenticity.

ABOVE Here the use of two stencils identical in outline, presents a realistic impression of patterned cloth. In this case the second stencil provides the striping over another that is only a bland outline.

LEFT Very regular bridging between the cut-away shapes helps to create the full impact of the central star shape. Making wide enough connecting pieces at the center of the star is important if the stencil is to give good service.

WALLS

Stenciling looks best on a surface of broken-up color rather than a single flat shade. I prepare the walls ahead of time by applying a variety of tones – often several different shades of one color of latex paint. You can get a very nice effect by painting your wall a single color then daubing over it with a piece of flannel or cotton rag dipped into paint of a fractionally lighter or darker tone.

FURNITURE

You can stencil directly onto a wooden surface that has been cleaned with soap and water, and even onto an existing painted surface as long as it is in good condition.

Alternately, you can start from scratch by painting the piece with latex covered by a coat of varnish, or harder-wearing gloss or eggshell. It is best to prepare the surface properly using a primer, undercoat and top coat. However, you can apply more than one shade to get a more unusual mellow effect, as long as you carefully rub each coat down with fine sandpaper. Pay special attention to the corners and edges, rubbing them harder to produce a worn effect. If you will be working on a door, box or chest make certain that all working parts like hinges and locks are in good order, and oiled, if necessary, before you begin painting. Usually, it is easier to stencil drawers and cupboard doors if you remove any protruding knobs and handles before painting.

The interiors of certain pieces of furniture like chests and desks lend themselves to being stenciled as well.

FABRICS

The techniques of spray stenciling can be transferred successfully to material that is not going to be washed frequently. Natural fibers such as cotton,

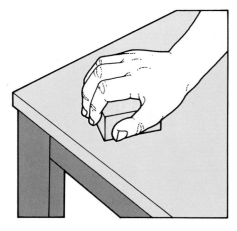

Wooden furniture can be given a more mellow effect if painted in one shade over another and sanded down between each coat.

If a fitting can't be removed, you should work your design around it for best effect.

Special small or cut-up stencils may be needed to accommodate fixtures or awkward areas.

Here, by incorporating the knob into the design, a much more pleasing effect is achieved.

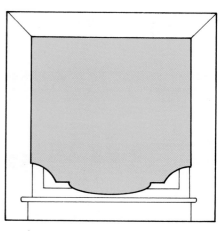

When anticipating stenciling on fabric, you should make up the pieces before applying any paint.

Hardwearing items like floor coverings can be strengthened by a final coat of varnish.

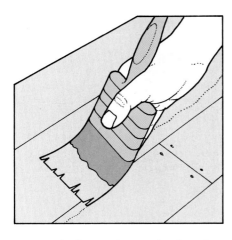

A wooden floor can be stripped and tinted with a thinned latex coat; a concrete floor must be thoroughly washed.

Small items such as tables or boxes look best with a single, simple, centrally-placed image.

More than one image can be used successfully – especially on less obvious areas of furniture.

linen and silk are ideal as they hold color well. However, colors are muted compared to other surfaces as fabric can soak up much of the paint.

FLOORS

Both concrete and wooden floors are ideal for stenciling. A concrete floor should be thoroughly washed clean. Stripped wooden floors can be covered with a thinned coat of water-based paint to eliminate the roughness of varnished boards. Or, a wooden floor in good condition painted in a complementary color, can be worked on directly. Both types of floor should have a minimum of three coats of matte or gloss clear polyurethane varnish applied; each coat allowed to dry for 24 hours.

PLACING YOUR STENCILS

If you are working with a single image it's best to situate this in the center of your surface. On a small item such as a box or table this is easy to determine with a tape measure. On a larger surface like a wall, however, the best way to find the center is to fix a pin into each corner of the wall or floor, and stretch two pieces of string diagonally from corner to corner. Mark the point where these cross with a piece of tape and center your image.

When painting a border, ensure that the entire top edge of your cut-out design is the same distance to the edge of the card. If it isn't, you may have to trim the card or add to it. Now you have a consistent depth guide. Start in one corner and work around the area – maintaining the desired distance from the edge. If you are working on a wall, use a vertical strip of masking tape to tape off the corners. Place the stencil into the corner and on the tape, pulling it firmly around and continue with your painting. This will guarantee a neat edge at the corner that won't interfere with the flow of the design. For

Borders can be used as panels to break up areas, frame doors or windows, or around an entire room.

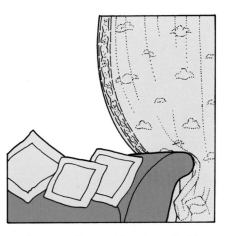

All-over stenciling provides a dramatic, rich effect on fabrics, walls or floors.

Stenciling can also be used to pull together a problem area, or coordinate disparate features.

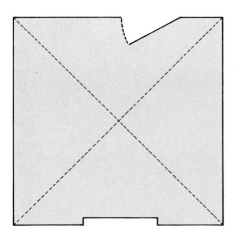

To place your stencil on the midpoint of a large area use string stretched diagonally from corner to corner.

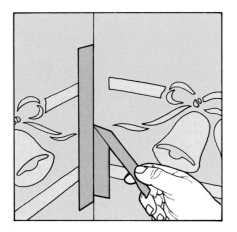

To ensure neat edges at corners, place strips of masking tape there, bridge with stencil, and spray.

When using aerosol adhesive cover the surrounding area with newspaper, and wear a mask and goggles.

bordering around certain areas – like a window or door – you will need a corner, and possibly, link pieces. Start again in the corner and work outwards. Use your link pieces to even out any awkward joints.

ATTACHING YOUR STENCIL

Stencils can be attached to any material – plaster, wood, fabric, metal, glass, etc. – but they need to be firmly fixed so that no paint sprays underneath and spoils the finish.

Aerosol adhesive provides an ideal way of attaching stencils. This coats the stencil's surface with a thin layer of adhesive that remains tacky for some time, and enables the stencil to be stuck down and lifted off several times.

To spray your stencil, position it reverse-side up on a sheet of protective paper. Spray the glue thinly and evenly all over it. Let it set a few minutes before placing it accurately, adhesive-side down, on your surface.

When working with aerosols, you should always follow the manufacturer's advice and make certain always to work in a well-ventilated area. Wear a cotton or paper mask that will protect you against breathing in the spray. Do not smoke or use it near a flame. Do not use the aerosol for any extended length of time and, if you are pregnant, avoid using it altogether.

If for any reason you want to reverse your stencil, you will have to deaden the glue by applying a film of talcum powder across its sticky surface.

Cheaper, and more readily at hand, pins can also be used. Tap them in lightly with a small hammer at intervals along the cut edges of the design – not the border. They should stand firmly but be easy to remove.

Small amounts of adhesive putty can be used when working on metal to hold the stencil. Apply them sparingly and press the stencil down firmly, ensuring close contact with the surface you are about to spray.

Pins should be tapped in lightly around the cut edges of the design to prevent paint seeping underneath.

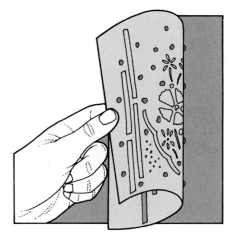

Small amounts of adhesive putty can be used when you are planning to spray onto metal.

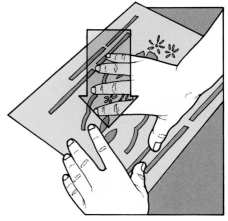

Whatever fixing material you use, make certain your stencil is in close contact with your surface.

Once the stencil is fixed, secure it further with small strips of masking tape around all edges.

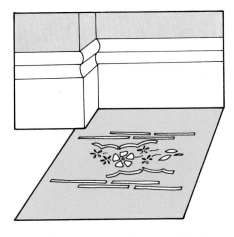

Occasionally, you may have to cut blank pieces of your stencil to make it fit certain restricted areas.

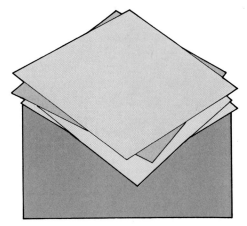

Rectangular pieces of card with strips of masking tape along one end make handy, reusable masks.

MASKING OFF

Once the stencil is placed, secure it with small strips of masking tape to keep it from moving while you are working. It may be necessary for you to cut off some blank areas of stencil in order to make it fit in restricted areas such as around corners or fixed handles and light switches. Then protect the surrounding area with paper held down with more masking tape. This will keep the paint from spoiling the neighboring areas.

If you are doing a lot of stenciling, it is worth making card masks.

APPLYING YOUR COLORS

Spray paint provides a hard, durable and lasting finish and the range of available colors can be extended by using them in combination. The paint is applied with a minimum of contact, thus ensuring the stencil is secure at all times. A wide variety of spray paint is available from art supply stores and automobile shops and you might like to make sure that the paints you are using contain no fluorocarbons, which are harmful to the ozone layer.

The technique to master is to apply the paint in a very fine spray – the barest film of color – and to achieve an end result that is produced by mixing and blending a variety of shades.

You should hold the can anywhere from 3 to 6 inches from the surface – for small details hold it closer, for larger areas further away. For the best results, hold the can at a slight angle to the surface. Use a gentle pumping movement on the button, and it is important that you move the can very slightly to produce a light sporadic spray. This will prevent paint building up in any one area. As you spray, the sound of the paint being released should be a gentle puffing. A prolonged, sharp sound means that you are pressing too hard and too long, and the paint will run.

Check the label of your spray paint to make certain it contains no fluorocarbons (no harmful elements).

Apply the paint in a light sporadic spray; gently pump the button, and move the can slightly and smoothly as you go.

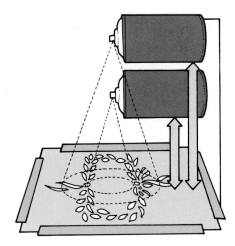

Hold the can closer for small details – about 3 inches away – and further back for larger areas – about 6 inches.

Use guards to direct your spray and to prevent colors from mixing where you don't want them.

Move your guard in whatever direction is necessary to cover or protect the different areas.

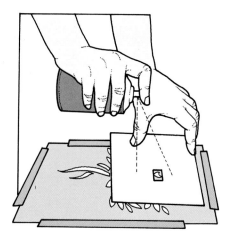

For very small areas of color you can spray through a small hole cut in a guard.

GUARDING

To keep colors from mixing where you don't want them, use small pieces of card – guards – to help direct your spray onto or away from areas. Keep the guard in your free hand and move it in whatever direction is necessary to cover the area that you wish.

Very small details can be painted through small holes cut in the card.

PAINT EFFECTS

It is advisable to limit the number of paints that you work with at any time. Beginners especially should restrict themselves to about four colors. But even with this small number you should be able to get an enormous range of effects by intermingling them; in fact, you will find it possible to create an incredible variety of colors and tones.

Even if you want a strong area of color, you must apply this in several layers rather than in one thick burst. A three-dimensional effect can be produced by combining faint and more densely-shaded areas.

Subtle blendings of color can also be achieved. You shouldn't worry about colors overlapping slightly onto neighboring shapes, as this will give your stenciling a more mellow look. Nor should you care about occasional splatters as these do look attractive so long as they are not thick blobs. Other effects can be achieved using shaped guards or more than one stencil.

DAUBING

On a plaster surface, such as a wall, I often prefer to soften the painted images by daubing them over with a light covering of white latex paint or the background color. This produces a more subtle final effect and integrates the stencilwork into the surface of the plaster. A good idea is to pour some

Spray through a guard that is unevenly torn around its edge, to produce a mottled effect.

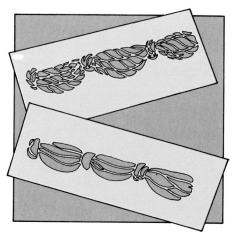

More than one stencil can be used with dramatic effect. A broadly cut stencil produces a fairly solid painted area.

A more finely detailed stencil can be superimposed and sprayed through in a darker shade.

Daubing over with white latex on a dampened, scrunched-up rag pleasingly softens the painted image on plaster.

A final coating of furniture polish can be used to integrate stenciling on a wooden surface.

To duplicate a stencil easily, lay it over another piece of card and spray through in a single shade.

paint into the lid of your paint can and use this as a palette. Then apply the paint with a damp, scrunched-up rag, patting it over the surface. Be a little cautious in the use of daubing as the paint will dry lighter than it appears at first.

FINISHING OFF

Completed walls, when they are dry, can be given a coat of water-soluble glaze as an overall protection. This glaze also eliminates the shine of the stenciled images. You must be certain to cover the entire area as any space left untouched will eventually discolor and be different from the rest.

Stenciled floors must always be covered in a polyurethane wood seal in either a gloss, satin or matte finish. Floor cloths should also be finished with a varnish coat.

Wooden surfaces, except for floors, can benefit from a final coating of furniture polish which allows the stenciling to integrate well with the surface. Polishing also brings out areas of color which reflect light. The polish should be applied after the item has been allowed to dry for ½ hour.

MAINTAINING STENCILS

Frequent handling can damage stencils as can an eventual heavy build-up of paint. If you are going to use a stencil repeatedly, you can easily make another copy. Lay the completed stencil over card of sufficient area. Spray the image with a single dark-colored paint. Then cut out the sprayed area.

Stencils do not need to be cleaned after use but they should be allowed to dry thoroughly after a heavy build-up of paint. Leave them in the open for at least a day; it is advisable to apply a small amount of powder to soak up any surplus glue.

Store your stencils in a cool, dry place, separated by sheets of card. Lay them flat on shelves, preferably.

Then, when it's needed, cut through the painted images to produce an exact copy.

Before storing a stencil it should be cleaned of any excess glue by dusting with talcum powder.

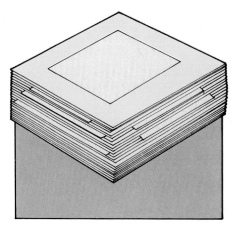

To store stencils properly, lay them flat and separate them by sheets of newspaper.

GLOSSARY

ANTIQUING – the artificial recreation of the patina of centuries past so as to create a charming effect of long use and wear.

BAIZE – a coarse woolen fabric napped to imitate felt.

BALLUSTRADING – a row of upright, often vase-shaped, supports, joined by a rail serving as an enclosure for staircases and balconies.

BASEBOARD – a wooden board placed at the junction of the floor and wall.

BERGÈRE CHAIR – an armchair with cane sides and back and a wide upholstered seat.

CAROLEAN – a term relating to the period of Charles I (1625–49). This period is known as Early Colonial in the United States.

CASTELLATED – having battlements and turrets like a castle.

CEILING-MEDALLION – a decorative molding through which a light fixture is suspended.

CHAISE LONGUE – strictly speaking, a full armchair with an extended seat that forms a leg rest. The term is now used to describe a couch with a back-rest at one end only.

CLEAR SHELLAC – a wood sealer that is used to protect and isolate any areas of stenciling that bleed.

COMBING – an ancient Egyptian method of wall painting, this method gives a stripy effect. It involves the use of a card with teeth cut out of it, dipped into an oil-based paint and 'combed' over the wall.

CORNICE – a structure, usually fitted across the top of windows, to cover the top edges of curtains. It can be made from wood or stiffened fabric mounted onto a board.

COVE CORNICES – if the detail is picked out in different colors, cornices give a finished and interesting effect at the point where the walls join the ceiling.

CREWELWORK – embroidery worked with slackly twisted worsted yarn.

DADO RAILS – originally devised to protect walls from the backs of chairs, these are usually about 3ft up the wall. They break up the wall visually, and you can even mimic a real dado rail with a stenciled frieze along the wall. The area below this rail or frieze is known as the dado.

DAG – an ornamental point, normally cut in the edge of a garment.

DECOUPAGE – the art of decorating screens, boxes, and other items of furniture with paper cut-outs covered with a clear glaze varnish.

DISTEMPER – a process of painting in which the pigments are added to a mixture of egg yolk, and size or egg white and which is used for scene painting or mural decoration.

DISTRESSING – creating the appearance of age or excessive wear on a piece of furniture by sponging and flicking oil glaze on to it with a stencil brush, and sometimes sanding it afterwards to roughen it even more.

DRAGGING – an effect of fine graduated lines pulled down the length of a wall with a large, long-haired brush; this technique gives an impression of height to a room.

DUST RUFFLE – a hanging border of drapery, normally found attached to a bed cover or made up as a separate item and placed underneath the mattress.

EGGSHELL LACQUER – a varnishing technique that creates the illusion of the spider's-web lines found on old oil paintings.

EMPIRE – the style of furniture popular in France from 1779–1815, and that corresponds to late Georgian in England and American Empire (1804–1815) in the United States.

FAUX BOIS – 'false wood' painting was practiced on pottery in the Bronze Age, and has been much used since in interior design as a background for trompe l'oeil. The effect of knotting and graining is also used to embellish furniture and sometimes to imitate inlaid marquetry.

FESTOON BLIND – made from fabric, ruched up vertical panels, remaining permanently gathered even when hanging down to their full length.

FRIEZE – A decorated band along the top of a room wall.

GEORGIAN – relating to the period of the reigns of George I, II and III of England (1714–1811). Early Georgian is 1714–1860, and Late Georgian 1760–1811. In the United States, part of the Georgian period, from 1750 onwards is known as Chippendale.

GLAZING – the effect of painting thin, almost transparent layers of color over others to produce a hard, shiny, glassy finish to the surface.

GOTHIC – characterized by pointed arches, and a style of architecture prevalent in Western Europe in the 12–14th centuries.

JACOBEAN – characteristic of the period of James I of England (1603–25).

LINEN PRESS – A large cupboard containing fixed or sliding shelves for linen storage, often mounted on a chest of drawers.

LINING-IN – fine single lines of contrasting colors are painted on furniture to emphasize the shape and detail of the features. A fast-drying opaque watercolor is one of the easiest paints to use with this method.

MARBLING – the technique of imitating marble; the various types of marbling are known as alabaster, brecciated, laminated, serpentine, statuary, travertine, and variegated.

MARQUETRY – decorative veneers laid together to form abstract or pictorial motifs. Veneers are most often made from exotic woods.

MASK – to protect or cover an area that surrounds a surface being painted.

PAISLEY – a type of pattern whose most characteristic feature is an ornamental device known as a cone.

PORTIERRES (DOOR CLOTHS) – these traditional tapestries were originally hung from door frames or draped in place of doors to keep out drafts. Door cloths of canvas, calico or sheets can look very effective when stenciled with fabric dye or paints.

RAG-ROLLING, RAGGING – a wall painting technique using a scrunched-up rag which is pressed into a wet glaze. Useful for lage expanses of wall, ragging works well with two or more soft tones used together, one on top of the other.

SCUMBLING – a typical 1930s style of painting using an opaque coat on top of a bright base coat.

SLEIGH BED – a style of bed most popular in the first half of the 19th century having a solid headboard and footboard that roll upward at the top.

SPONGING – a quick method of making a soft cloudy effect with a sponge dipped in paint, this also works well using two colors, which creates a more marbled effect.

STAY-BARS – these strengthen the weak spots in a stencil, serving to hold it together when working with large areas and rounded motifs. In the past, the Japanese also kept their stencils firm by laying human hairs between two sheets of oiled stencil paper in a mesh-like structure.

STIPPLING – applying paint with a brush to give a speckled appearance similar to the effect made by the pointillist painting technique of the French Impressionists.

STUMPWORK – a traditional form of needlework practiced in the 15th to 17th century. It originally incorporated elaborate raised embroidery using various materials that were raised up by stumps of wood. It now forms a source of inspiration for some of the stencils in this book.

SWAG – a garland suspended between two points.

TEMPLATE – a thin, often metal plate used as a guide for cutting out and tracing stencils.

TOILE DE JOUY – an 18th century French scenic pattern usually printed on cotton, linen, or silk in one color on a light background.

TROMPE L'OEIL – a painting technique meaning 'a trick of the eye', this is used to create an impression of perspective by the use of shadows and highlights. Paneling, baseboards, cornices and dado rails make ideal areas for trompe l'oeil.

VAULTED CEILING – an arched structure of masonry.

VICTORIAN – contemporary with or typical of the reign of Queen Victoria (1837–1901).

WHITEWASH – A substance made from lime and water used for whitening a surface instead of paint.

SUPPLIERS

All of Lyn Le Grice's designs are available in the United States. You may order them from The Stenciler's Emporium.

The Stenciler's Emporium
P.O. Box 6039
Hudson, OH 44236-6039

(216) 656-2827

In England, kits and the following stencil supplies can be ordered through Stencil Design Limited.

Stencil supplies:
Lyn Le Grice
Stencil Design Limited
Bread Street
Penzance, Cornwall TR18 2EQ

(Telephone: 0763 69881)

Many of the materials mentioned in the text can be found at stationery, hobby and hardware stores, and artists' suppliers, such as:

Pearl Paint Co. Inc.
308 Canal Street
New York, NY 10013

(212) 431-7932
(800) 221-6845
Mail order service

Charrette Corporation
215 Lexington Avenue
New York, NY 10016

(212) 683-8822

MAIL ORDER ADDRESSES

Most do offer catalogs
Call or write for more information

The Stenciler's Emporium
P.O. Box 6039
Hudson, OH 44236-6039

(216) 656-2827

Stencil House of New Hampshire
P. O. Box 109
Hooksett, NH 03106

(603) 625-1716

My Secret Garden
45 Broadway
P. O. Box 333
Greenlawn, NY 11740

(516) 754-6935

Decorative Arts Studio
R.R. 1, Box 136, Route 30
Dorset, VT 05251

(802) 867-5915
Catalog available

Hand Stenciled Interiors
590 King Street
Hanover, MA 02339

(617) 878-7596

Stencil World
222 East 85th Street
New York, NY 10028

(212) 517-7164
Catalog is $3.00

The Stencil Shoppe, Inc.
6 Olde Bridge Village
Chadds Ford, PA 19317

(215) 459-8362
Two catalogs available – supplies or stencils

Bayberry Stenciling
12710 124th Street, Court East
Puyallup, WA 98374

(206) 848–4780
Custom design studio and mail order
Catalog available

RETAIL STORES

which carry various stencil products

Anne's Folk Art
3967 B Pacific Coast Highway
Torrance, CA 90505

(213) 375-1814

Country Stenciler
120 South Main Street
Doylestown, PA 18901

(215) 340-1740

The Olde Rose Stencil and Gift Shoppe
Fort Eddy Road
New Hampshire Highway Hotel
Concord, NH 03301

(603) 228-5228

The Quilter's Corner
119 Forest Hill Road
Macon, GA 31210

(912) 474-5879

Berry Mountain Shop
Two Pleasant Street
Laconia, NH 03246

(603) 524-4868

Piper Classics
R.D. 2, Box 145
Pipersville, PA 18901

(215) 766-0331

Covered Bridge Arts and Crafts
449 Amherst Street
Nashua, NH 03063

(603) 889–2179

Country Charms
1425 South MacArthur
Springfield, IL 62704

(217) 546-2244

Jeanne Benson Decorating Arts Center
142 West Monroe
Kirkwood, MO 63122

(314) 822-7412
Call for catalog information

To find the name of a store in your area which carries basic stencil products, you may call toll free:

Stencil Ease
New Ipswich, NH

(800) 633-5700

In the United States, a non-profit organization exists which is designed to benefit anyone interested in the art of stenciling. For information about membership, please write to:

Stencil Artisans League, Inc.
P.O. Box 920190
Norcross, GA 30092